The Observer's Book of
STEAM LOCOMOTIVES
OF AUSTRALIA

The Australian Observer's Series

- A1 SNAKES AND LIZARDS
- A2 BIRDS
- A3 STEAM LOCOMOTIVES
- A4 CIVIL AIRCRAFT (incl. New Zealand)
- A5 SAILING CRAFT (incl. New Zealand)
- A6 ROCKS AND MINERALS

The Observer's Book of
STEAM LOCOMOTIVES
OF AUSTRALIA

DAVID BURKE

METHUEN OF AUSTRALIA
SYDNEY

FREDERICK WARNE (PUBLISHERS) LTD
LONDON: NEW YORK

ACKNOWLEDGEMENTS

I would like to thank Mr G. L. Johnson, F.C.I.T., for his considerable assistance in the compiling and checking of the locomotive data contained in this book. My appreciation is also extended to individuals and officials of railway enthusiast organizations, and railway departments, who helped by providing many of the illustrations to be found in these pages. Picture credits are listed in the final pages.

DAVID BURKE

First published in 1979 by
METHUEN OF AUSTRALIA PTY LTD
301 Kent Street, Sydney
225 Swan Street, Richmond
91 Elizabeth Street, Brisbane
6 Sherwood Court, Perth

© David Burke 1979

This book is copyright. Apart from any fair dealing
for the purposes of private study, research, criticism
or review, as permitted under the Copyright Act, no part
may be reproduced by any process without written permission.
Inquiries should be addressed to the publishers.

National Library of Australia
Cataloguing-in-Publication data
Burke, David.
   The observer's book of steam locomotives of Australia.
   (The observer's series)
   Index.
   ISBN 0 454 00078 2
   1. Locomotives—Australia. I. Title. (Series)
625.261'0994

First published in Great Britain 1979 by
FREDERICK WARNE (PUBLISHERS) LTD
ISBN 0 7232 1652 5

Printed in Hong Kong by
Dai Nippon Ptg Co. (H.K.) Ltd
Typeset by Queensland Type Service Pty Ltd

CONTENTS

Acknowledgements	iv
Preface	vii
Introduction	1
Locomotives of the . . .	
Victorian Railways	15
New South Wales Railways	49
Australian National Railways Commission	97
Central Region	99
Northern Region	125
Tasmanian Region	137
Queensland Railways	150
Western Australian Government Railways	174
Private railways	199
Museums and enthusiast lines	217
Appendix A Wheel Classification	232
Appendix B The Loco Builders	234
Photograph Sources	238
Glossary	239
Index of Locomotive Classes	243
General Index	247

"No other product of man's mind has ever exercised such a compelling hold on the public's imagination as the steam locomotive. No other machine in its day has been a more faithful friend to mankind or contributed more to the cause of industrial prosperity in this, the land of its birth, and throughout the world. No other machine somehow is so gentle, and yet when unleashed is capable of such noble power and strength . . . nothing quite so graceful in action and nothing quite so romantic.

"Those who have lived in the steam age of railways will carry the most nostalgic memories right to the end."

> R. F. Hanks, speaking at the naming ceremony of the "Evening Star", the last steam locomotive to be built for British Railways, at Swindon, Wilts, 18 March 1960.

PREFACE

Australian railways once operated a force of 3493 steam locomotives; this was the official count at the end of World War II.

Locomotives of the hills, of the plains, of the city lines, of the outback country branches; of the shunting yards, of dingy colliery sidings, of the great express routes, of steep cogwheel slopes. Steam locomotives that clattered across high iron bridges; that rattled by suburban backyards, liberally spraying Monday's washing with their soot; that rambled across the Nullarbor; that plunged into black tunnels filled with swirling smoke. Locomotives of troop trains, of wheat trains, of mineral trains, mail trains, mixed trains; of the Sunshine and the Spirit, Overland and Australind, the Flyer and the Fish; locomotives of the dawdling weekly goods, of fast fruit specials, of the seaside excursion train; locomotives that made haunting whistle sounds across the valley on a cold, frosty night.

In an eruption of steam and smoke and the smell of warm oil, they began in 1854 and for about a century chuffed and puffed and clink-clonk-clanked across the nation. Many of them were the proud machines of Australian design, the C38 and the S-class Pacifics, the Mountain class 500s and D57s, and Heavy Harry 4-8-4. Untold hundreds were built in Australian workshops, Ipswich and Islington, Eveleigh, Newport, Cardiff and Clyde, with skills that have now disappeared. And driven and fired on rolling footplates in the glare of red-white flame with a certain magic that has just about escaped us.

As much as any of man's machines of transport—more than most, perhaps—the steam locomotive helped to make Australia possible.

Then, in the 1950s, the diesel-electric arrived, and in

a few short years the steam locomotives were so many hunks of lifeless iron. Only a few remain: reminders of the glory that was steam.

The Observer's Book of Steam Locomotives of Australia reviews the motive power of each railway system in three groupings: passenger engines; goods engines; and miscellaneous tank engines—crane locos, tram motors and so on.

The listing is essentially of those steam engines that can still be *observed*. Some, fortunately, are in operating condition, thanks to the labours of enthusiast volunteers and the co-operation of railway departments and private industry; others stand on static display in railway museums or can be found in suburban parks and country towns.

Because of their significance to Australian locomotive development certain other classes have also been included although, regrettably, they have been completely scrapped. Many more engine types no doubt are worthy of selection from the ranks of the non-observable; those that appear are the result of personal choice and the limitations of our pages.

INTRODUCTION

From Homemade to "Heavy Harry"

Australia's first steam locomotive, if one should dignify it by such a name, was a rudimentary four-wheel machine, combining the frame of a ballast wagon with a 4-hp pile-driver engine.

The nation's second locomotive was equally homemade but rather more innovative. James Moore, engineer of the Melbourne and Hobson's Bay Railway Company, drew up the plans, and the local foundry of Messrs Robertson, Martin and Smith completed it (according to a report of the day) "in a space of time

Artist's impression of the Melbourne and Hobson's Bay passenger engine of 1854.

RAILWAYS OF AUSTRALIA:
Main State Networks

- operating line
- line under construction
- inoperative line

Track Gauges

762 mm (2 ft 6 in)	Victoria
1067 mm (3 ft 6 in)	Queensland, South Australia, Western Australia, Northern Territory, Tasmania
1435 mm (4 ft 8 ½ in)	New South Wales, Victoria, South Australia, Western Australia
1600 mm (5 ft 3 in)	Victoria, South Australia

The isolated lines in north-west Western Australia are private iron ore haulage systems of 1435 mm (4 ft 8 ½ in) gauge.

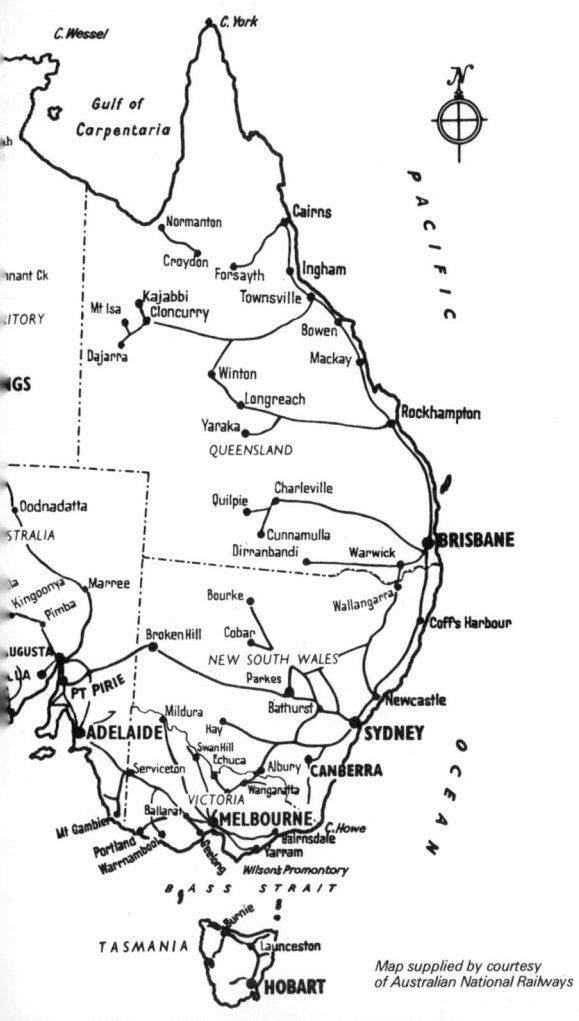

under ten weeks, little longer than is usually allowed in England".

English locomotive deliveries were a sore point with the directors of the Hobson's Bay Company in that year of 1854. Four locomotives ordered from the works of Robert Stephenson and Company were seriously overdue; with capital of £200,000 already raised (double the original estimate) they urgently needed to service that investment with revenue—hence the decision to make railway engines in an infant colony where none had been seen, let alone built, before.

On 12 September Australia's first steam railway began operation between Flinders Street Melbourne and The Beach at Sandridge (now Port Melbourne). Crowds cheered by the lineside; Lieut-Governor Sir Charles Hotham, R.N. and Lady Hotham waved back; and the James Moore locomotive puffed doggedly off to cover the 3.6-km (2¼-mile) route in just under ten minutes. From what can be reconstructed of its appearance, the Moore locomotive was a 2-2-2T (single driving wheel—tank) type with unprotected footplate and an output of 30 hp; on a trial run three days before the opening it had impressed Hobson's Bay officials by pulling 132 tonnes (130 tons) at 40 km/h (25 mph). Cost of the engine was £2500.

The Melbourne *Herald* reported next day: "The engine performed its work well, and was tolerably punctual in its trips. But as the six o'clock train was leaving Sandridge a slight derangement occurred which prevented its progress, so that passengers had to alight and walk up to town. The stoppage was understood to arise from some of the firebars having fallen out, so that the fire could not be sustained, or immediately relighted."

On Christmas Day 1854, the first of the overdue Stephenson locomotives entered service, the Moore engine having been completely unworkable since 1 December and even the little pile-driver model,

Locomotives outside old Sydney Station sheds in the mid-1870s.

utilized during earlier breakdowns, apparently beyond recall. Named "Melbourne", "Sandridge", "Victoria" and "Yarra", the imported Stephenson 2-4-OT* type represented the first trickle of an enormous British influence which, though gradually diminished in later years, was to continue for a century, right through the great steam era of the Australian railways.

Steam never lost its capacity to draw a crowd, to inspire and thrill with the mighty sight and sound of whirling siderods, the pant of air pump, the thunder of exhaust. The great 4-8-4 "Heavy Harry", largest locomotive ever built by the Victorian Railways, was in a manner a direct descendant of the original James Moore engine that first clattered across the same 1600-mm (5 ft 3 in) gauge. Where the Hobson's Bay engine was midget, the H220 was mighty in every way—three cylinders, 100-kg (220-lb) boiler pressure, a mammoth auto-stokered firebox and a 12-wheel welded tender with capacity for 9.1 tonnes (9 tons) of coal and 63 644 litres (14,000 gallons) of water. H220, completed at Newport Workshops in 1941, represented

---

* For an explanation of wheel classification see Appendix A, p. 232.

perhaps the epitome of national steam-locomotive design, drawing on a heritage of British and American practice, yet, more importantly, merging them both in a tradition that had become essentially Australian.

Was the writing on the wall for steam, even in those urgent days of World War II when every item of locomotive power was forced into Herculean service? H220's companion locomotives were never built, the Western line to the South Australian border on which it was to haul the Adelaide express, the Overland, never strengthened. Instead H220 saw out its days as a goods engine, a lone black goliath nightly wheeling fast freight along the North-East line to Wodonga, the only route that had been sufficiently reinforced to support its 264-tonne (260-ton) weight.

Steam belonged to the break-of-gauge years, when Sydney- and Melbourne-bound interstate trains halted irrevocably at Albury for the cry of "All change here!"; when a journey to Perth from the east, according to the particular period of history, carried all the agonizing

Queensland B13-class 4-6-0s double-heading a mixed train in the early days of the Great Northern Railway.

connotations, once Adelaide was reached, of broad gauge to Terowie, narrow gauge to Port Augusta, standard gauge to Kalgoorlie, narrow gauge beyond... almost unbelievable in a later age of through-gauge diesels. In those days it was inconceivable that Western Australian flatcars might appear in South Brisbane or Victorian wagons be unloaded in Perth; that an Australian National Railways Commission might form to encompass Commonwealth, Tasmanian Government and South Australian country systems. Bounded by broken-gauge borders and mostly inward-looking State administrations, by the local dictates of geography, traffic and money—or the lack of it—Australian steam power developed as that of six quite foreign States. For the nation, it might be a transportation scene full of inefficiency and economic nightmares; for the enthusiast—great!

Even when they shared a common rail-gauge width, such as Victoria and South Australia (1600 mm—5 ft 3 in), Queensland and Western Australia (1067 mm—3 ft 6 in), no two State systems designed a common steam loco class. (There were a couple of well-known exceptions, such as the narrow-gauge ASG Garratt of World War II.) Apart from using the same basic wheel arrangements, such as 4-6-0 (ten-wheeler), 4-6-2 (Pacific), 4-8-0, or 4-8-2 (Mountain) which were among the best known on larger types, none built locomotives that looked even remotely similar (again with the exception of some imports from the same overseas manufacturer).

None of the departments had the same rules of operation: arrangement of controls differed, as did location of fittings and methods of classification. On the broad and standard gauges, locomotives reached maximum size and power in the period between the mid-1920s (e.g., South Australia's 500 and 600 classes) and the early 1950s (the N.S.W.R.'s Beyer Garratt). Compared with locomotives in other parts of the

Ga-class No. 19, fitted with feedwater heater, heading the "Trans" in 1938.

world, and dictated by the confines of an often tight loading gauge and light trackwork with numerous sharp curves, the largest Australian locomotive at steam's peak usage would rank internationally as "medium big power"—a boiler pressure averaging around the 91-kg (200-lb) mark, passenger driving wheel diameter rarely more than 1.8 m (6 ft), tractive effort varying from 13 608 kg (30,000 lb) to 27 216 kg (60,000 lb).

Grate areas of the largest manually fed passenger locos—all Pacifics—challenged the fireman's skill and endurance; grate sizes were 4.4 m^2 (47 sq ft) on the C38 (N.S.W.), 4.6 m^2 (50 sq ft) on the S (Vic.), and 5.1 m^2 (55 sq ft) on the 600 (S.A.). With a 508-tonne (500-ton) express train, over a period of 60 minutes, a fireman would be required to feed some 1905 kg (4200 lb) of coal, a rate of about seven 4.5-kg (10-lb) scoopfuls a minute, into the blistering firebox on a swaying footplate.

British and American practice combined in producing the distinctive outlines of Australian locomotives; in contrast, few inroads were made by continental builders. Superheating and Walschaert valve gear were common features. Standard equipment included powerful electric headlights and the automatic coupler on larger gauges. Such devices as boosters, mechanical stokers and cross-compound pumps were adopted on latter-day engines. All State systems used the cowcatcher (or pilot), with the exception of New South Wales which fitted them only for use on unfenced outback lines.

All States used the Westinghouse air-brake, with the exception of the Western Australian and Tasmanian 1067-mm (3 ft 6 in) gauges, which adopted vacuum brakes.

Australia's locomotives were predominantly coal-burners, but the locomotive coal of the various States being of vastly different quality, the Victorian and South Australian mainliners drew largely on the Maitland pits of New South Wales, which produced a

Three stages of S.A.R. passenger development: (left) Rx-class 4-6-0, (centre) 520-class 4-8-4, (right) 620 Pacific.

rapid-steaming coal. Industrial unrest at the mines in the late 1940s forced a hurried conversion of many locomotives to oil (shunters also burnt firewood), though only a few classes endured as oil-burners. Victoria alone adopted the German Wagner self-cleaning front end—the "basher"—with its flower-pot funnel and smokebox deflector plates, either full length or in abbreviated form. The Victorian Railways experimented with the German Stug equipment for burning pulverized Yallourn brown coal on an X and an R class locomotive. Because of poor-quality local fuel, South Australia was unusual in employing a system that combined coal and oil combustion, the tenders carrying both oil tanks and conventional bunkers.

Australian steam-locomotive engineers showed little tolerance for compounding, apart from experience with a few imports around the turn of the century. The simple three-cylinder principle was reserved for three notable designs, the H and S of Victoria and the D57-D58 of New South Wales, the S and D57-58s being remembered for a somewhat alarming gooseneck in the lead driving axle to accommodate the motion of the inside connecting rod. On N.S.W. metals, experiments began on a C36 class with a Giesl oblong ejector, distinguished by a long narrow stack—alas, too late to bring a reward for efficiency in steam's declining years.

Many big-wheel express locomotives were capable of high speeds, at least in theory: the Victorian S class were reputedly designed for 193 km/h (120 mph) and in N.S.W. the C38, which had the State's maximum 1753-mm (5 ft 9 in) driving wheel, was regarded as a "100 mph machine". But in service, track condition severely restricted passenger speeds to an official 113-km/h (70-mph) top in New South Wales and Victoria, and 97 km/h (60 mph) in South Australia and on the then Commonwealth "Trans" line. Bursts of 129 km/h (80 mph) were attained in tests, and it is not hard to find veteran enginemen with stories of hair-raising "unofficial" records that went far beyond any figure the Chief Mechanical Engineer would permit. Victoria again was the only system to keep a check on its whole fleet of road locomotives by fitting Flaman recorders which incorporated speedometers and a removable paper tape.

The British practice of naming locomotives was never widely popular although all States have dabbled in it—New South Wales with a few C36s and C32s used on the Blue Mountains, Illawarra, Newcastle and South Brisbane runs in the 1930s; Victoria with the four Spirit of Progress S class, and South Australia, the most persistent of the three, culminating with its streamlined 520 class 4-8-4s carrying the names of prominent citizens. In Western Australia certain locos were given names of State rivers and mountains. From

Construction of a heavy freight X-class 2-8-2 at Newport Workshops, Melbourne, in 1929.

widespread popularity in the last century, the use of colourful liveries and highly polished boilerwork declined. Most spectacular of the modern large power were Victoria's four blue S class for the Spirit; New South Wales cloaked some of its C36s and C38s in an appealing green livery; South Australia tried American-style silver frosting on the smokebox doors of its 500Bs and 720s; while in the final years Queensland locos suddenly became resplendent in green, blue and brown, according to class and roster.

Narrow-gauge locomotives belonged mostly to the light-power bracket. Low-weight rails and primitive bridges restricted axle loads, while a crippling loading gauge prohibited heavy designs comparable with the 1067-mm (3 ft 6 in) monsters of South Africa.

Queensland, with the largest narrow-gauge stable of some 850 locomotives, had no non-articulated class exerting a greater tractive effort than 10 886 kg (24,000 lb) until the arrival of the Beyer Garratts in 1950.

Long-nosed cowcatchers and brass boiler rings are remembered as the trade marks of Queensland locomotives, while on the far side of the continent the utterly dissimilar Western Australian locos were mainly noted for clean, well-proportioned "British colonial" outlines. Both Queensland and Tasmanian locomotives had the regular screw coupler and side buffers; those made for the narrow gauges of Western Australia, South Australia, and, formerly, the Commonwealth, had the rather sinister-looking "meat chopper" centre buffer and draw-hook gear. All States used the side-tank locomotive for both suburban trains and shunting, but only Queensland and Western Australia, with busy steam-operated city lines, developed the design through the 1940s to keep pace with traffic requirements.

What sight or sound of steam quite equalled four N.S.W. locomotives lifting a 2032-tonne (2000-ton)

Two N.S.W.R. standard goods assist a D57 on the coal traffic out of Lithgow.

coal train from the floor of the Lithgow Valley? In majestic procession those iron horses came, three pulling in front and one banking at the rear, the thunder of their stacks echoing between beetling rock walls, the mushroom plume of smoke darkening the sky, the great connecting rods rising and falling with each measured beat. The leading locomotives were standard goods 2-8-0s and a third D50 type as pusher at the rear, while the train engine was a superb D57 or D58, the 232-tonne (228-ton) Mountain type that reigned as king of the Blue Mountains grades until electrification displaced it almost overnight. They were the days of steam!

The C38 (right) pacing V.R.'s R class on broad gauge at the 1964 visit of the Pacific to Melbourne.

VICTORIAN RAILWAYS
1854

Though the Victorian Railways did not commence operation until 13 January 1859, almost three and a half years after the N.S.W. Government system, pride of place in any Australian locomotive history is usually accorded the southern colony, for it was there on the short Hobson's Bay Company line between Melbourne and Sandridge that Australia's first steam railway began.

Private railways played an important part in the early expansion of Victoria; some of them, so to speak, never raised a puff, or inevitably yielded their fond hopes to government control, as did that very genesis of the V.R., the Melbourne & Mt Alexander Railway Co. Each of the surviving private concerns had its own locomotive shopping list, and the history of the colonial system has been made all the more colourful by the comings and goings of a host of tiny engines. Who else but the Geelong & Melbourne Co. (opened 25 June 1857) would identify its motive power with such names as "Titania", "Oberon", "Samson" and "Tubal-Cain"? (No mere numbers would do!) In Melbourne itself the locomotive proliferation, especially of tank types, went ahead, with the growth on the south suburban side alone of six small companies which ultimately amalgamated into the Melbourne and Hobson's Bay United, continuing as such until the government takeover of 1879.

For the locomotive observer, however, the ages of particular significance begin with the administration of Richard Speight, first Chairman of Commissioners, who instituted an advanced policy of "standard"

Artist's impression of the V.R. locomotive power on the first train from Ballarat to Creswick in 1874.

engine types in the late 1880s when the V.R.'s iron-horse stable amounted to no less than twenty-two different classes, plus several engines of nondescript background. (Locomotive Superintendent Solomon Mirls had first begun classifying engines by letters of the alphabet in 1886.)

Speight was ex-Midland Railway Co., and his leaning was strongly English and particularly towards Kitson & Co. of Leeds, who quickly supplanted that traditional supplier, Beyer, Peacock. The "Kitson era" resulted in pattern engines and designs for six classes of clean-lined British-style locos, among them the Y 0-6-0, the E 0-4-2 and the New A 4-4-0; they appeared in rich green livery with smart lining out, domes and boiler bands of highly polished brass, and shining copper funnel caps. These and other classes were built by that other phenomenon of Victorian locomotive history, the highly accomplished Phoenix

First goods loco on the Victorian government system, No. 11 (formerly No. 2), a George England 0-6-0.

Foundry of Ballarat which from 1873 to 1904 constructed a total of 361 engines, all but nine for V.R. service.

Though Victoria had sometimes shopped from U.S. motive-power catalogues, the appointment of Mr (later Sir) Thomas Tait, a former assistant general manager of the Canadian Pacific Railroad, as Chairman of Commissioners in 1903 ushered in a new wave of North American influence, particularly on appearance as apart from design. This was apparent in a rich Canadian red livery and a cab of full footplate width with a side door to the running plate above the driving wheels.

But the modern genius of V.R. engine power remains Alfred E. Smith, who, as Chief Locomotive Designer and later Chief Mechanical Engineer, brought out of Newport Workshops (where 536 engines were built up to 1962), and the ancillary V.R. shops of Ballarat North and Bendigo, an impressive fleet of heavy and light line classes. In these, as with Speight of the previous century, efficient standard designs were the aim. Of these engines we best recall the utility DD 4-6-0; it is followed by that stalwart ten-wheeler, the A2 of double-headed Overland fame; the heavy freight X-class Mikado; and, perhaps best remembered, the four S class of 1928–30 which were later to supply the engine power of Sir Harold Clapp's sleek Spirit of Progress. The story goes that A. E. Smith asked Sir Harold why a new loco was needed to haul his pet streamliner "when two A2s will do the job just as well". One assumes that Sir Harold smartly told Mr Smith to get back to his drawing board! Ironically, eight years after the S class had disappeared prematurely to the scrapheap, two Walschaert A2s in gleaming black were coupled together for the final run of the Spirit on broad gauge before the diesels, now to be standard gauge, resumed.

Australia has seen many notable steam locomotives, but the observer may well ask himself if any iron horse has generated quite such public excitement as accompanied the shrill call of the chime whistle and the urgent beat of three-cylinder exhaust when the S-class Pacific took to the rails with the Spirit of Progress in far off 1937.

Gauge 1600 mm (5 ft 3 in)

PASSENGER TYPE

1861   B Class   2-4-0

Regarded as the first main-line passenger power on the Victorian Railways, the original 26 B-class locomotives were acquired in 1861–3 when construction of the lines to Ballarat (via Geelong) and Bendigo was in hand.

Beyer, Peacock and R. & W. Hawthorn of England built these famous high-wheeled locomotives with their wide-topped balloon funnels, massive outside frames bolted around 76-mm (3-inch) thick oak beams and "over-arm" connecting rods. They were fitted with the unusual Cudworth divided firebox, with two fire-doors,

An "over-armer", the V.R.'s 2-4-0 B-class express engine, imported from England in 1861–2.

to gain maximum heat from the wood fuel at first in use.

The B class were regarded as fast and easy steamers and an additional six were ordered from Beyer, Peacock in the next year. A final two were built locally by Phoenix Foundry, Ballarat, but with conventional fireboxes. The Bs were eventually replaced by larger express locomotives and withdrawn in the early 1900s. No. 88 hauled the first Sydney express from Albury to Melbourne on 20 August 1883, while No. 72 was assigned to the return express next day. Unfortunately no survivor of the class remains for exhibition.

Principal dimensions

Driving wheels	6 ft 0 in	1829 mm
Cylinders	16 × 24 in	406 × 610 mm
Pressure	130 lb (psi)	896 kPa
Weight	64 tons	65 tonnes
Tractive effort	8,875 lb	4026 kg

Built 1861–81

The 4-4-0 express fleet of the V.R. included "Old A", "New A" and "AA" types; 544 was a "New A".

1884 A Class 4-4-0

Three similar classes of 4-4-0 locomotives were acquired for main-line passenger working during the 1880s. The first, almost identical to N.S.W.'s D 255, was later known as the Old A class and the 10 members were built by Beyer, Peacock in 1884. They were rebuilt with more powerful boilers from 1900 and were scrapped during the 1920s.

To achieve greater tractive effort, next came the 16 (New) A class of which Kitson & Co. supplied a pattern engine in 1889; 15 were built at Phoenix Foundry of Ballarat between 1889 and 1891. They shared duties with the older A class on main-line trains and were eventually relegated to country branches.

In 1900 a further 20 of an improved design known as the AA class were supplied by Phoenix Foundry; the final batch had bogie tenders. All three types were gradually supplanted by the more powerful A2, and members of the original A classes had been withdrawn and scrapped by the early 1930s.

Principal dimensions
Driving wheels   6 ft 0 in   1829 mm

Cylinders	18 × 26 in	457 × 660 mm
Pressure	175 lb	1207 kPa
Weight	75 tons	76.2 tonnes
Tractive effort	15,120 lb	6858 kg

Built 1884–1903

1902   D3 Class   4-6-0

The first of A. E. Smith's ubiquitous DD locomotives, completed in 1902, was to be the forerunner of over 260 class members built until 1920. Intended for the main line, the DD was soon displaced by larger power and then became a most useful light-line mixed traffic locomotive, working all over the Victorian system. Builders were Newport Workshops (138), Ballarat Workshops (8), Bendigo Workshops (8), Baldwin Loco Works (20), Walkers Ltd (20), Beyer, Peacock (20), Thompsons (Castlemaine) (40) and Phoenix Foundry (7).

The DDs, numerically the largest V.R. class, were later divided into types D1 (pictured), D2 and D3.

Fitted with superheaters and larger boilers, the D3s operated passenger and mixed trains until the diesel era.

The DDs were reclassified in 1922 as D1 class (saturated with 457-mm (18-inch) diameter cylinders), D2 class (superheated) and D3 class (rebuilt superheated with larger boilers). A derivative tank version (D4 class) was also built for suburban service. (See p. 44.)

Withdrawal of the D1 started in 1929, although members of the D3 class continued in service for many years. The former Commissioner's Engine (D3) 639 has been retained while D2 class 604 and D3 class 635 are displayed at Williamstown Rail Museum. Other D3s displayed in the State are located at Maryborough (646), Swan Hill (688), Hamilton (659), Seymour (684), Bayswater (663), Beaufort (641), Bendigo (619), Lismore (671), Rosebud (638, 640), Ringwood (677), and Stawell (607).

Principal dimensions
Driving wheels	5 ft 1 in	1778 mm
Cylinders	19 × 26 in	483 × 660 mm
Pressure	170 lb	1172 kPa

Weight	100 tons	101.6 tonnes
Tractive effort	22,200 lb	10 070 kg

Built 1902–20

1907   A2 Class   4-6-0

A small-engine policy maintained during the late nineteenth century found the Victorian Railways without adequate motive power to meet the needs of expanding interstate and country passenger services in the early 1900s. One of the first products of a locomotive design section under A. E. Smith was the A2 ten-wheeler, which proved to be among Australia's most successful express classes.

The A2 was destined to handle virtually all major main-line passenger workings as well as selected freight tasks for well over 45 years. Of clean, elegant appearance, with large-diameter driving wheels, the first 125 A2s were built at Newport Workshops between 1907 and 1915; they were all equipped with Stephenson's inside valve gear.

The handsome A2, one of Australia's best-known 4-6-0 passenger types.

The Walschaert valve gear equipped second batch of A2 ten-wheelers.

In 1915 the design was changed slightly with the adoption of Walschaert's outside valve gear for a further 60 locomotives which were built at Newport, Ballarat and Bendigo shops between 1915 and 1922. Various modifications were made over the years including superheating, modified "basher" front ends that resulted from E. E. Brownbill's experimental trials, fitting of smoke deflector plates, and larger tenders.

Eventually the A2 was replaced on crack express duties by larger 4-6-2 and 4-6-4s, although they continued to haul important country trains right to the end.

The class was withdrawn starting in 1946. Two have been preserved at the Railway Museum, Williamstown —995 and 888. Two others are on static display at Echuca (996) and Warragul (986).

Principal dimensions
Driving wheels	6 ft 1 in	1853 mm
Cylinders	22 × 26 in	559 × 660 mm
Pressure	(Walschaert) 185 lb	1276 kPa
	(Stephenson) 200 lb	1379 kPa

Weight   121 tons   122.9 tonnes
Tractive effort   27,100 lb   12 247 kg

Built 1907–22

1928   S Class   4-6-2

Without doubt the legendary S class would be one of the finest locomotives both in appearance and performance ever to grace the Australian railways. The four class members were built at Newport between

The S class, unstreamlined but with smoke deflectors, at Spencer Street in the 1930s.

1928 and 1930 to the design of A. E. Smith, then Chief Mechanical Engineer. They were intended for fast passenger express working, and immediately replaced the smaller A2 on the Sydney express.

Introduced without streamlining, they incorporated many advanced design features, including three cylinders. With the launching of the crack air-conditioned Spirit of Progress in 1937, the four locomotives were named and transformed with a streamlined casing and covered front end and the addition of large tenders mounted on two six-wheel bogies for the 306-km (190-mile) non-stop run to Albury.

In 1952 they were converted to burn oil, but soon afterwards the B-class diesel-electrics supplanted them on top passenger working.

They were progressively scrapped as boilers became due for renewal. The last in service, class leader 300, was withdrawn in late 1954. Regrettably, none of these fine locomotives was preserved. The S 300 was named "Matthew Flinders"; the S 301, "Sir Thomas Mitchell"; the S 302, "Edward Henty"; and the S 303, "C. J. Latrobe".

In streamlined garb and with 12-wheel tender, the S was assigned to the Spirit of Progress in 1937.

Principal dimensions
Driving wheels	6 ft 0 in	1829 mm
Cylinders (3)	20½ × 28 in	521 × 711 mm
Pressure	200 lb	1379 kPa
Weight	224 tons	227.6 tonnes
Tractive effort	41,675 lb	18 903 kg

Built 1928–30

The V.R.'s R class, the only express 4-6-4 Hudson type operated in Australia.

1951   R Class   4-6-4

Intended to replace the ageing A2 class generally on fast passenger services, the 70 R class were built by the North British Locomotive Co. of Scotland.

First designed as a Pacific (4-6-2), they appeared as a 4-6-4—the only class of tender locomotive in Australia with the Hudson wheel arrangement.

The design included a mechanical stoker and roller-bearing axle boxes on both locomotive and tender, as well as SCOA-P type driving wheels to facilitate the possibility of conversion to standard gauge. After a few minor problems, the R class settled in as an efficient, fast-moving machine. However, the introduction of diesel power soon displaced them from the main passenger services such as the Overland, yet they performed just as effectively on freight trains.

The class was fitted for oil firing in 1955–7 and one equipped with Stug brown-coal-burning apparatus in 1954, but they were converted back to conventional fuel three years later. The Rs were withdrawn after a comparatively short life; No. 704 has been preserved at the Williamstown Museum. Two, 707 and 761, have been held for vintage train and fan excursions; 766 has been preserved at Bendigo.

Principal dimensions

Driving wheels	6 ft 1 in	1853 mm
Cylinders	21½ × 28 in	546 × 711 mm
Pressure	210 lb	1448 kPa
Weight	187 tons	190 tonnes
Tractive effort	32,080 lb	14 551 kg

Built 1951–2

GOODS TYPE

1873   T Class   0-6-0

Representing conventional English inside-cylinder design, the T class was a mixed-traffic locomotive. The first five were built by Beyer, Peacock in 1873 and these were followed by 18 from Phoenix Foundry in 1884. A further four from Beyer, Peacock joined the

T-class 0-6-0: its final years were spent shunting.

Victorian Railways when the privately owned Deniliquin–Echuca line was acquired in 1923.

The Ts served on lightly trafficked lines for many years and also operated as shunters on sharply curved sidings. Withdrawals commenced in the 1920s, two remaining in service until 1951. T94 is preserved at Williamstown.

Principal dimensions

Driving wheels	4 ft 3 in	1295 mm
Cylinders	16½ × 20 in	419 × 508 mm
Pressure	160 lb	1103 kPa
Weight	56 tons	56.9 tonnes
Tractive effort	13,660 lb	6169 kg

Built 1873–85

1885   Y Class   0-6-0

The Y class belonged to Commissioner Speight's plan for standard motive power. It was introduced for heavy goods service with a pattern engine from Kitson

The Y-class shunter, an 1889-vintage 0-6-0, lasted until 1960.

& Co. in 1885; 30 more were built by Phoenix Foundry in 1888–9.

The Ys followed contemporary British design and were regarded as big locomotives in their time. Originally confined to main lines, they were later transferred to the branches, yet were sufficiently versatile to handle the longer-distance suburban and excursion trains as well as freights. Final tasks found them in yard and workshop shunting and on suburban goods. Y108 has been retained at Williamstown Rail Museum.

Principal dimensions

Driving wheels	4 ft 6 in	1372 mm
Cylinders	18 × 26 in	457 × 660 mm
Pressure	175 lb	1207 kPa
Weight	74 tons	75.2 tonnes
Tractive effort	21,840 lb	9906 kg

Built 1885–9

1900 V Class 2-8-0

To improve on the small six-coupled locomotives then in use, the Victorian Railways ordered a pattern 2-8-0 from Baldwin Works, U.S.A., in 1899. This handsome typically American freight machine was unique in having four cylinders powered on the Vauclain compound system. A further 15 were then built by Phoenix Foundry in 1901–2, allowing the V to assume heavy freight duties throughout the State.

Though it was an effective locomotive, the compound method was frequently improperly used by drivers who could control the entry of high-pressure steam to the low-pressure cylinders on heavy grades at the expense of boiler-operating efficiency and the fireman's labours. As a result, fuel and water saved by compounding were offset by higher maintenance costs;

Phoenix Foundry built 15 of the heavyweight American 2-8-0 V class.

this led to a decision in 1912 to convert the locos to two simple cylinders.

The impressive V class exerted an influence on other freight designs of later years. They ran until the boilers began to wear out in the 1920s, and were progressively withdrawn, the last in 1930.

Principal dimensions

Driving wheels	4 ft 6 in	1372 mm
Cylinders	$18\frac{1}{2} \times 26$ in	470×660 mm
Pressure	180 lb	1241 kPa
Weight	88 tons	89.4 tonnes
Tractive effort	23,730 lb	10 764 kg

Built 1899–1902

1918   C Class   2-8-0

Described as the most powerful locomotive class in Australia when introduced, the first C appeared from Newport Workshops in 1918. The tough consolidation type was intended to handle heavy-tonnage fast freights on the main country and interstate routes.

Consolidation C5 was first on the V.R. to carry a cross-compound air pump.

Between 1918 and 1926 Newport built a further 25.

As with the contemporary A2 passenger locos, considerable improvements were made over the years to the C class to lift performance. These included a modified front end, electric lighting and smoke deflectors.

From 1946 the Cs were converted to burn oil when serious coal shortages occurred in the State. It is worth noting that during World War II they were also assigned to some heavy passenger trains.

The introduction of main-line diesel-electrics nudged the C class off the heavy freights, and from 1954 on all but one were scrapped. No. 19 is at the Williamstown Museum.

Principal dimensions

Driving wheels	5 ft 0 in	1524 mm
Cylinders	22 × 28 in	559 × 711 mm
Pressure	200 lb	1379 kPa
Weight	128 tons	130 tonnes
Tractive effort	38,400 lb	17 418 kg

Built 1918–26

1922   K Class   2-8-0

The K class was the first of the V.R.'s "modern" light-axle-load locomotives for country lines when smaller, obsolete power was overdue for replacement. Newport Shops built the first 10 Ks in 1922–3; the class was later improved with modified front ends, smoke deflectors and cross compound air compressors. The same design was also adopted for a further 43 locomotives urgently needed during World War II and completed at Newport between 1940 and 1946.

The 2-8-0 K, designed as the original light-lines utility class of 1922.

Used throughout the State on goods trains, the K was also assigned to limited passenger working when speed allowance was raised from 72 km/h (45 mph) to 80 km/h (50 mph). In the late 1950s the onslaught of branch-line diesels signalled the withdrawal of the Ks, although several have been preserved, including No. 165 at Williamstown, 177 at Ararat, 163 at Frankston, 169 at Korumburra, 191 at Wangaratta, 170 at Wonthaggi, 167 at Wycheproof, 154 at Moe, and 181 at Numurkah. Two were retained by the V.R. in working order for special trains (153 and 184).

Principal dimensions

Driving wheels	4 ft 7 in	1397 mm
Cylinders	20 × 26 in	508 × 660 mm
Pressure	175 lb	1207 kPa
Weight	104 tons	105.7 tonnes
Tractive effort	28,650 lb	12 995 kg

Built 1922–46

1925 N Class 2-8-2

The moves towards a national uniform gauge prompted the Victorian Railways, back in the 1920s, to design an N-class Mikado to light-line specifications yet suitable for conversion to a 1435-mm (4 ft 8½ in) gauge. Although much of their equipment was identical to the K-class 2-8-0s, the new engines differed in having a trailing axle to support a firebox that would be high enough to accommodate standard-gauge axles. An order for 30 Ns was completed by Newport between 1925 and 1931.

In 1930, class-leader 110 received a Franklin two-cylinder booster (auxiliary engine) for the trailing truck, which lifted tractive effort by 5,750 lb. Sub-

N 110, the only light-line 2-8-2 to be equipped with a booster engine on the trailing truck.

sequent improvements were made during the 1930s, and the design was again adopted for 50 locomotives acquired under the post-war Operation Phoenix programme in 1945–50; this time North British was the builder. Ten Ns of the second batch were sold to the South Australian Railways soon after acquisition to meet a motive-power shortage on that system, and these were known as 750 class. A proposal to build 20 more at Newport in 1950 was cancelled after only three had been completed.

The last of N class, No. 432, is now on display at Williamstown, the rest of the class being withdrawn during the 1960s.

Principal dimensions

Driving wheels	4 ft 7 in	1397 mm
Cylinders	20 × 26 in	508 × 660 mm
Pressure	175 lb	1207 kPa
Weight	124 tons	126 tonnes
Tractive effort	28,650 lb	12 995 kg

Built 1925–51

1929   X Class   2-8-2

The Mikado wheel arrangement was also selected for Victoria's new heavy-freight motive power, again to be convertible to standard gauge. For some years after introduction they were chiefly used on goods trains that travelled after dark and were dubbed the "night owls".

Based somewhat on the earlier C class, the X handled the bulk of heavy main-line traffic for many years, with the exception of Gippsland lines.

The locos were all built at Newport Workshops: 11 in 1929–30 and 18 between 1937 and 1947. The X had a large free-steaming boiler, and all but one were

The V.R.'s most powerful regular freight loco, the 2-8-2 X class.

equipped with a booster. Certain modifications upgraded the X-class performance; in 1949 No. 32 was equipped to burn pulverized brown coal. Although they were robust engines, the advent of high-horsepower diesel-electrics put an end to further development of heavy steam. The X class was scrapped between 1957 and 1961; No. 36 is preserved at Williamstown.

Principal dimensions

Driving wheels	5 ft 1 in	1549 mm
Cylinders	22 × 28 in	559 × 711 mm
Pressure	205 lb	1413 kPa
Weight	185 tons	188 tonnes
Tractive effort	38,700 lb	17 554 kg
with booster	48,300 lb	21 908 kg

Built 1929–47

1941   H Class   4-8-4

To eliminate double heading on Melbourne–Adelaide passenger expresses in the late 1930s, the Victorian Railways decided to build three huge locomotives to be known as H class. The first was steamed at Newport in 1941 and immediately received the nickname of "Heavy Harry", which was to be much better known than its number (H220). It was announced as the heaviest and most powerful steam loco in Australia.

Although intended for the Serviceton line, the locomotive was never used in the West, owing to limited bridge capacities between Melbourne and Ararat. Instead H220 was assigned to the North-East, hauling express freights between Melbourne and Wodonga. Plans to complete the other two H class were never fulfilled, and 220 remained as the sole class member. On a few occasions it was also tried on crack North-East passenger trains, including the Spirit of

The V.R.'s largest loco, the 4-8-4 "Heavy Harry".

Progress. Design features incorporated in H220 included power-operated reverse gear, mechanical stoker, duplex blast pipes and three cylinders. The 6.3-m^2 (68 sq ft) grate was the largest of any Australian locomotive—bigger by a small margin than the areas of other massive freight auto-stokered types, such as N.S.W.R.'s D57/58s and Garratt and S.A.R.'s 500B. Withdrawn in 1958, "Heavy Harry" is on display at the Williamstown Rail Museum.

Principal dimensions
Driving wheels   5 ft 7 in   1702 mm

Cylinders	21 × 28 in	533 × 711 mm
Pressure	220 lb	1517 kPa
Weight	260 tons	264.2 tonnes
Tractive effort	55,000 lb	24 948 kg

Built 1941

1953 J Class 2-8-0

Steam's last throw in Victoria was another light-line design suitable for turning on 16.1-m (53-ft) turntables. Introduced as part of the post-war motive-power programme, the J-class locos suffered the fate of being delivered concurrently with the diesels. Obviously they were destined for a short working life.

Based on the earlier K class 2-8-0, the J had a distinctive high-pitched boiler and a firebox set above the frames, another design feature to equip them for easy conversion to standard gauge. Sixty were built by Vulcan Foundry, half as oil burners, half for coal. The J was used mainly on freights and passenger trains

J-class No. 559, last V.R. steam loco to enter service.

on lighter country lines. Though considered a most useful class, they went to the scrapheap commencing in 1967. Those Js retained include No. 556 at the Williamstown Museum and several in country towns—No. 536 at Colac, 524 at Donald, 512 at Alexandra, 539 at Dimboola, 550 at Mirboo North, and 507 at Yarrawonga.

Principal dimensions

Driving wheels	4 ft 7 in	1397 mm
Cylinders	20 × 26 in	508 × 660 mm
Pressure	175 lb	1207 kPa
Weight	113 tons	114.8 tonnes
Tractive effort	28,120 lb	12 755 kg

Built 1954

TANK AND MISCELLANEOUS TYPES

1873–1910   F Class   2-4-2T

Seeking motive power for short passenger trains on lightly trafficked lines, the Victorian Railways looked to the modification of small 2-4-0 tender locomotives which had been supplied originally between 1873 and 1880. Seven of these F class were rebuilt into 2-4-2T (tank) engines at Newport Workshops in 1910 and reclassified as "F Motors"—a designation which related to the passageway (on three of the locos) through the divided coal bunker to enable crewmen to enter the train to collect tickets. The engines were withdrawn by 1926, though No. 178 remained as a boiler-washout unit at North Melbourne Locomotive Depot until 1951. No. 176 was sold to Sunshine Harvester Co. in 1920 for works shunting duties. In

The F motor, a small 2-4-2T, once hauled Melbourne's legendary Deepdene Dasher.

1961 it was donated to the Williamstown Rail Museum where it is now on display.

Principal dimensions

Driving wheels	5 ft 0 in	1524 mm
Cylinders	16 × 20 in	406 × 508 mm
Pressure	160 lb	1103 kPa
Weight	42 tons	42.7 tonnes
Tractive effort	10,580 lb	4799 kg

Built 1910–11

1878   M Class   4-4-0T

With 4-4-0T wheel arrangement, the first of this class was a pattern engine from Beyer, Peacock in 1878. Of conventional English appearance, it was front runner for new suburban power, and the design was adopted for a further 21 units ordered from Phoenix Foundry.

In the 1900s the engines were rebuilt into the ME class 4-4-2Ts, having more water and coal capacity

The M class, a 4-4-0T of 1878, later converted to 4-4-2T, known as ME.

and increased power. When the larger DDE-class 4-6-2T locomotives took over, all were withdrawn during the 1910–20 period.

Principal dimensions

Driving wheels	5 ft 0 in	1524 mm
Cylinders	17 × 20 in	432 × 508 mm
Pressure	140 lb	965 kPa
Weight	40 tons	40.6 tonnes
Tractive effort	11,464 lb	5200 kg

Built 1878–86

1889 E Class 2-4-2T

A motley collection of locomotive types was hauling Melbourne suburban traffic when the E class appeared in 1889. Intended as a Speight standard design for suburban duty, the class was built for two-way running with leading and trailing axles and four driving wheels.

(Above) a familiar sight in Melbourne yard—the 0-6-2T version of the E-class tank.

(Below) An E-class 2-4-2T in Melbourne steam suburban traffic—electrification displaced steam in the 1920s.

After the first E class, a pattern engine supplied by Kitson & Co., contracts for a further 45 were placed with the Phoenix Foundry, Ballarat, and for 25 with David Munro & Co. of South Melbourne.

The E class ran principally on the more level inner-suburban lines until electrification. Twenty were sold to the South Australian Railways in 1920, while 24, classified EE, were rebuilt to the 0-6-2T arrangement for shunting duties. The 2-4-2Ts were scrapped from the 1920s on, the last, No. 506, being withdrawn in 1953. The 0-6-2Ts went longer, the last surviving until 1963; of these, No. 506 (still carrying its original number, 236) is to be seen at Williamstown.

Principal dimensions

Driving wheels	5 ft 0 in	1524 mm
Cylinders	17 × 26 in	432 × 660 mm
Pressure	140 lb	965 kPa
Weight	53 tons	53.8 tonnes
Tractive effort	14,000 lb	6350 kg

Built 1889–94

1893   Z Class   0-6-0T

The first locomotive to be built at Newport Workshops in 1893 was a diminutive Z "Goods Motor", No. 526, intended for very short freight trains. When train loads grew too heavy, the steam motor was returned to Newport in 1904 and converted to a crane locomotive, having a 3-tonne (3-ton) swivelling crane mounted over the boiler and a four-wheeled tender attached.

Officially listed as No. 3 crane, or "Polly", it was used at various workshops including around North Melbourne Carriage and Wagon Shops, and also attended many suburban derailments. It is preserved at Williamstown.

Newport pioneers of 1893, the 0-6-0 Zs sported a "boxed-in" cab appearance.

Principal dimensions

Driving wheels	3 ft 6 in	1067 mm
Cylinders	12 × 22 in	305 × 559 mm
Pressure	140 lb	965 kPa
Weight	24 tons	24.4 tonnes
Tractive effort	8,976 lb	4071 kg

Built 1893

1908   D4 Class   4-6-2T

Confronted with a continual need for more powerful tank locomotives on suburban passenger operations, the Victorian Railways chose the highly successful DD class tender engines as a basic design. The first D4 class was completed by Newport Workshops in 1908, to be followed by a further 57 up till 1913.

Originally classified as DDE, they were designed for eventual conversion to tender form when suburban electrification took over, although only two were altered in this way. The DDE was used on the steeper

The D4 tank—still handsome despite the later addition of shunter's sideboards.

suburban lines until the spread of electrification in the 1920s, when they were put on minor passenger, suburban goods and shunting duties. The D4 classification was given in 1929. Some were later fitted with superheaters, and cowcatchers at both ends for semi-country operations to Mornington and Werribee. Their final years were occupied in the yards with shunters' footboards extending outside the driving wheels on each side. Stable and free-running, they were finally replaced by larger steam and diesel locomotives during the 1950s. No. 268 has been retained at Williamstown Rail Museum.

Principal dimensions

Driving wheels	5 ft 1 in	1549 mm
Cylinders	18 × 26 in	457 × 660 mm
Pressure	185 lb	1276 kPa
Weight	69 tons	70.1 tonnes
Tractive effort	20,100 lb	9117 kg

Built 1908–13

Narrow gauge 762 mm (2 ft 6 in)

1898   Na Class   2-6-2T

Near to the turn of the century the Victorian Railways planned a network of narrow 762-mm (2 ft 6 in) gauge lines as a means of providing low-cost transport in sparsely populated parts of the State. To obtain

Na 3, the first narrow-gauge loco produced at Newport.

suitable motive power on the steeply graded routes, the V.R. contracted with Baldwin Locomotive Works in 1898 for the supply of two tank-style locos.

Additional engines having the same "American" appearance were completed by Newport Workshops between 1900 and 1915 as more of the small railways were opened. In all 17 were built, and they proved to be trouble-free with the exception of two which used the compound principle. Classified Na, the fussy 2-6-2Ts were extremely hard-working and could handle large loads over steeply graded and sharply curved tracks of often indifferent quality—albeit at the low speed of usually no more than 23 km/h (15 mph).

The narrow-gauge lines gradually succumbed to rising costs and falling traffic, and were closed from 1952 onwards. Today only the Belgrave–Lakeside section of the Gembrook line remains in operation, and then only through the efforts of the Puffing Billy Preservation Society which maintains and runs the service. Six Na class have been retained for operation on the Puffing Billy line—Nos 3, 6, 7, 8, 12 and 14.

Principal dimensions

Driving wheels	3 ft 0 in	914 mm
Cylinders	13 × 18 in	330 × 457 mm
Pressure	180 lb	124 kPa
Weight	34 tons	34.5 tonnes
Tractive effort	13,000 lb	5897 kg

Built 1898–1915

1926 G Class 2-6-0 + 0-6-2

The only Garratt locomotives acquired by the Victorian Railways were two G class, No. 41 and No. 42, which were purchased for the 762-mm (2 ft 6 in) gauge lines based on Moe and Colac. They were built by Beyer, Peacock & Co. to supplement or replace the smaller Na class. The trim Garratts eliminated double heading

G 42, one of two 1926 Garratts ordered by the V.R. for the narrow gauge.

and proved very effective until both lines were closed in the 1950–60 period. No. 41 was scrapped in 1964, but No. 42 has been retained by the Puffing Billy organization at Belgrave, where consideration is being given to the possibility of returning it to traffic.

Principal dimensions

Driving wheels	3 ft 0 in	914 mm
Cylinders	$13\frac{1}{8} \times 18$ in (4)	333×457 mm
Pressure	180 lb	1241 kPa
Weight	70 tons	71.1 tonnes
Tractive effort	25,280 lb	11 467 kg

Built 1926

NEW SOUTH WALES RAILWAYS 1855

The "first government-owned railway in the British Empire" opened between Sydney and Parramatta on 26 September 1855—exactly twenty-five years and eleven days after the coming of the world's first steam public railway, the Liverpool-to-Manchester line in England. One might also recall another famous September date thirty years before that gala New South Wales event—15 September 1825, the opening date of George Stephenson's first public steam line from Stockton to Darlington in the north of England.

If a thumbnail sketch of railway history is to be given a correct interpretation, it should be pointed out that the infant N.S.W. system, in the shape of those 22.4 km (14 miles) of track to Parramatta, apparently

Assembly of a Robert Stephenson 0-4-2 in Wilson's Paddocks at Chippendale, 1855.

lay at the root of the break-of-gauge insanity which was to plague Australian rail operations for a hundred years and at the same time inhibit and complicate the development of the Australian steam locomotive. The N.S.W. line (which had just transferred to government control) opened to standard gauge, but in the critical planning years before 1853 the Irish engineer of the then ailing Sydney Railway Company, F. W. Shields, persuaded his directors to alter the construction plans from the already selected standard width to the Irish broad gauge of 1600 mm (5 ft 3 in). Shields abruptly resigned over a salary reduction, and his successor, James Wallace, a Scot, proved a staunch adherent of Stephenson's 1435 mm (4 ft 8½ in). It was to this gauge that the English rolling-stock suppliers were contracted to build.

Unfortunately, however, the Victorian and South Australian companies' equipment was already ordered to comply with Shields' 1600 mm (5 ft 3 in), and having made an earlier alteration from the British Colonial Office's recommended uniform gauge to suit N.S.W., they could not—or would not—change; thus was a Frankenstein's monster of the rails let loose.

One might ask if the less developed colonies of Queensland, Western Australia, South Australia (in part) and Tasmania (as a second choice) would have decided on their 1067-mm (3 ft 6 in) gauge for any reason other than economy. The fact remains that the established disunity of railway practice between the senior colony and the south added weight to the argument for a narrow gauge.

In every direction from Sydney away from the coast, the early railway builders were faced with barriers of steep sandstone escarpments—in the Blue Mountains to the west, where grades were to reach 1 in 33; in the tablelands and Great Divide to the south; and to the north, where there was the added difficulty of crossing the great Hawkesbury River. And beyond the mountain

Australia had few single-wheelers: the 2-2-2 express T14 of 1865 was one.

ridges lay the vast undulating distances of a sparsely populated interior. These geographic and economic realities were to influence the type and variety of engines embodied in the motive-power programme, from the small Stephenson 0-4-2s of 1855 to the final chapter of the AD60 class Garratts, six times the weight of those first machines.

Many men were responsible for guiding the locomotive policy of the N.S.W. railways; among them we must list the great builder himself, Engineer-in-Chief John Whitton, who in thirty-two years supervised the addition of more than 3300 km (2051 miles) to the colonial system. W. Thow, of the London & North Western, came via the South Australian Railways to assume the post of Locomotive Engineer and Chief Mechanical Engineer. He is best remembered for his distinctive "porthole" cabs on the long-serving loco classes with which his name, and that of his Chief Draughtsman, J. Scoular, are associated—the C32 and the standard goods. E. E. Lucy was architect of the big power leading up to the early 1930s, when 1423 steam locomotives were on the N.S.W. roster—his administration as C.M.E. was notable for the C35 and C36 express ten-wheelers, and climaxed with the Mountain type D57. And there was Harold Young, under whose leadership appeared that final glory of fast N.S.W. steam: the C38 Pacific.

Gauge 1435 mm (4 ft 8½ in)

PASSENGER TYPE

1855   Class 1   0-4-2

Now housed at the Sydney Museum of Applied Arts and Sciences, "No. 1" locomotive of N.S.W. is a Robert Stephenson 0-4-2 which was one of the four original passenger locomotives unloaded at Campbell's

"No. 1", one of the four locos imported from Robert Stephenson in 1855.

Wharf, West Circular Quay, in January 1855. The dismantled sections were hauled on wagons to Wilson's Paddocks, Chippendale, where they were assembled for preliminary use in ballast and construction work. No. 1 is reported to have been steamed for the first time to Newtown on 29 March 1855.

On the opening day of the line to Parramatta, No. 3 drew the first passenger train while No. 2 took the Vice-Regal special under the control of Driver William Sixsmith and Fireman William Webster, the senior enginemen of the infant system. (No. 1 was not used at the inauguration, due to maintenance requirements.) Known as Class 1, the mixed-traffic 0-4-2s were quite large and advanced for the times. The old Sydney Railway Company's English consulting engineer, J. E. McConnell, adapted them from his powerful 0-6-0 goods type introduced to the London & North Western Railway in 1854.

Over the years, the true identity of No. 1 has been the subject of some debate, as rebuilding had taken place utilizing the parts of its companion pioneer No. 2.

Principal dimensions

Driving wheels	5 ft 6 in	1676 mm
Cylinders	16 × 24 in	406 × 610 mm
Pressure	120 lb	827 kPa
Weight	45 tons	45.7 tonnes
Tractive effort	8,900 lb	4037 kg

Built 1854

1870   M36 Class   0-4-2

When additional locomotives were required in the late 1860s, the N.S.W. Railways Department ordered four more of the original 1 class which had been purchased in 1855 to open the first line from Sydney to Parramatta. Having slight modifications to the earlier design, these

The Redfern-built No. 77, close copy of the original N.S.W.R. 0-4-2.

were listed as 36 class, and were built in Sydney by Mort & Co.

In 1870, when the first four 1855 locomotives were ready for withdrawal, another four locomotives of almost similar design were built at the railway workshops using the tenders of the original locomotives. All were withdrawn and scrapped between 1891 and 1904 except No. 78, which was retained for construction work. In 1928 No. 78 was officially retired and honoured by being placed on a plinth for public inspection at the Enfield Locomotive Depot. It has since been removed to the Rail Transport Museum at Thirlmere.

Principal dimensions
Driving wheels	5 ft 7½ in	1714 mm
Cylinders	17 × 24 in	432 × 610 mm
Pressure	125 lb	862 kPa
Weight	52 tons	52.8 tonnes
Tractive effort	10,800 lb	4899 kg

Built 1870–7

1877 Z12 Class 4-4-0

With almost 70 members, this was the first N.S.W. locomotive class to be built in large quantity. An adaptation of an earlier 2-4-0 with the addition of a leading four-wheel Bissell truck, the design was in turn based on a very successful 4-4-0 tank locomotive which Beyer, Peacock & Co. supplied to the Metropolitan Railway in London. Herman Lange, works manager and successor to Charles Beyer when the founder of the famous locomotive works died in 1876, is said to have personally supervised the development

Preserved Z12-class 1243 of the original 79 class, first built in 1877–9.

of the Australian eight-wheeler; 68 were built in four years with the first 30 from Beyer, Peacock, and later deliveries from Dubs & Co. in Scotland, Beyer, Peacock & Co., and the Atlas Engineering Works in Sydney.

Known initially as C79, they handled all "through" passenger and mail trains on the system for 20 years, but were later replaced by heavier and more powerful 4-4-0s and 4-6-0s. Twenty were converted to tank engines and became the CC79 (later Z14) class. The locomotives were finally relegated to outback un-ballasted lines and similar light duties. Two members, Nos 1219 and 1243, have been retained at the Rail Transport Museum at Thirlmere. No. 1243 carries its original number 176 which it was given for vintage train working. The first locomotive to work on the Queanbeyan–Canberra branch, No. 1210, has been displayed by the National Capital Development Commission at Canberra station.

Principal dimensions

Driving wheels	5 ft 6 in	1676 mm
Cylinders	18 × 24 in	457 × 610 mm
Pressure	140 lb	965 kPa
Weight	61 tons	62 tonnes
Tractive effort	13,000 lb	5897 kg

Built 1877–82

1882   Z15/Z16 Class   4-4-0

Important express-type locomotives in the early days of inter-colonial services were known as "High Flyers", of which three class variations existed. With inside cylinders and 1867-mm (6ft 1½ in) diameter driving wheels, these machines were used extensively on fast passenger trains in the 1880s and 1890s, including the early Melbourne Express, and then performed valuable banking or pilot duties as assistant locomotives to the more powerful P class during the early twentieth century.

They were eventually reduced to less demanding tasks on country lines, and were scrapped during the 1930s. Several were sold to industrial users.

Of 47 "High Flyers", the first six D255s, later known as the Z15 class, came from Beyer, Peacock in 1882, and conformed to a design which had proven very popular in the U.K. As "Old A", the same design was

A "High Flyer" of the 1880s, No. 255 was the class leader from Beyer, Peacock.

delivered to the Victorian Railways 1600-mm (5 ft 3 in) gauge. Subsequent deliveries were made to N.S.W. by Dubs & Co. They were swift and impressive locomotives, and the sight of a "High Flyer" in later years double-heading a P class on the evening mails and expresses over the steep grades to Hornsby was one to remember. Regrettably, no examples have been preserved.

Principal dimensions

Driving wheels	6 ft 1½ in	1867 mm
Cylinders	18 × 26 in	457 × 660 mm
Pressure	140 lb	965 kPa
Weight	64 tons	65 tonnes
Tractive effort	13,000 lb	5897 kg

Built 1882–6

1887 Z17 Class 4-4-0

The 17 members of this class of shapely locomotives were supplied by Vulcan Foundry in 1887 for service on steeply graded sections of the Northern line to Newcastle and the Illawarra line to Kiama. They were built with extended smokeboxes which allowed hard driving without blocking the lower boiler tubes with

A Vulcan 4-4-0 with outside cylinders, No.381 is sole survivor of the Z17 class.

ash. Harsh riding qualities made them unpopular with crewmen and they were soon replaced on main-line duties by more powerful 4-6-0s. They subsequently led uneventful lives on branch lines until all but one were withdrawn during the 1950s and 1960s.

The sole surviving member was retained for vintage train working and its number (1709) restored to the original No. 381. It is at the Thirlmere Rail Transport Museum.

Principal dimensions
Driving wheels	5 ft 6 in	1676 mm
Cylinders	18 × 26 in	457 × 660 mm
Pressure	140 lb	965 kPa
Weight	75 tons	76.2 tonnes
Tractive effort	14,200 lb	6441 kg

Built 1887

1892 C32 Class 4-6-0

Few experts would dispute that the C32 ten-wheeler is probably the most successful and enduring locomotive class ever introduced onto Australian metals. Designed by the then Locomotive Superintendent, W. Thow, the first 50 were delivered in 1892–3 from Beyer, Peacock. The P6, as they were called, were intended as motive power on fast passenger and mail trains. The 1524-mm (5-ft) driving sheets made them eminently suitable for steeply graded main-line sections as well as for dependable time-keeping on level tracks. Over the

The P6 (later C32) as equipped with bogie tender for the Melbourne Express.

next 19 years the class grew to number 191 locos with deliveries from Beyer, Peacock (106), Baldwin (20), Clyde Engineering (45) and Eveleigh Works (20). Bogie tenders were introduced and all eventually had superheaters fitted.

With the distinctive "porthole" cab sides, the grand C32s frequently reached speeds over 112 km/h (70 mph), no mean feat for a machine of their type. The design was also copied for the first passenger locomotives (G class) built for the then Commonwealth Railways' Trans-Australian line across the Nullarbor Plain. After 70 years' running in N.S.W. many were still performing well on major trains right up to the time of replacement by diesels.

Growing old graciously: a C32 in later years, equipped with electric headlight.

Three are on display at the Rail Transport Museum at Thirlmere—Nos 3203 and 3214 in working order while 3265 has been earmarked for exhibition by the Museum of Applied Arts and Sciences. No. 3237 is at a depot in Cowra.

Principal dimensions

Driving wheels	5 ft 0 in	1524 mm
Cylinders	21 × 26 in	533 × 660 mm
Pressure	160 lb	1103 kPa
Weight	110 tons	111.8 tonnes
Tractive effort	26,000 lb	11 793 kg

Built 1892–1912

1909 C34 Class 4-6-0

Many of the features of the C32 class were adapted for the five C34 4-6-0 express locomotives built by Eveleigh Workshops in 1909–10. These larger boiler engines were used mainly on the South line based at Junee and earlier as N928 class on the North Coast. Besides driving wheels of larger diameter than the C32, they

The C34 class: an "improved" ten-wheeler from Eveleigh Workshops in 1909–10.

also had Allan straight-link-motion valve gear, which C.M.E. Thow favoured. None of the class has been retained.

Principal dimensions
Driving wheels	5 ft 9 in	1753 mm
Cylinders	21 × 26 in	533 × 660 mm
Pressure	180 lb	1241 kPa
Weight	109 tons	110.7 tonnes
Tractive effort	23,900 lb	10 841 kg

Built 1909

1914   C35 Class   4-6-0

The late Con Cardew, an eminent loco engineer, once described the C35 as "the first considerable class of N.S.W. express locomotives of which it could be truthfully said that the conception, and general and detail design, were entirely the work of the Locomotive Branch design staff".

Intended to eliminate double heading over difficult sections, which was necessary with the smaller C32, E. E. Lucy's machine, as built, appeared with a distinctive Great Western Railway look—cut-away cab sides and stepped running boards. A total of 35 were constructed at Eveleigh Workshops between 1914 and 1923.

G.W.R. influence was especially evident when the NN 1027 was decked out for a Royal Train.

Initially identified as NN class, they acquired the nickname of "Nannies" (sometimes "Naughty Nannies"), which stuck throughout their working life. Early performance problems were overcome and the class was greatly improved by modifications made

The rebuilt C35 became one of the most useful N.S.W.R. passenger locos.

from 1938 with heavier frames, enclosed cabs and a valance below the running board.

They appeared at first on all main lines but were eventually concentrated in the northern part of the State, working much of the heavy passenger and express traffic as well as some fast freights on the Main North and North Coast. Diesels replaced them during the 1950s and 1960s. No. 3526 is located at the Rail Transport Museum, Thirlmere.

Principal dimensions

Driving wheels	5 ft 9 in	1753 mm
Cylinders	22½ × 26 in	572 × 660 mm
Pressure	180 lb	1241 kPa
Weight	145 tons	147.3 tonnes
Tractive effort	29,000 lb	13 154 kg

Built 1914–23

1925 C36 Class 4-6-0

Continuing its success with well designed and pleasingly proportioned passenger motive power, the Railway Department produced a new express type in 1925, specifically to achieve long journeys without changing locomotives and for 160-km (100-mile) non-stop runs. Though consideration was given to a Pacific type, they appeared as 4-6-0s, bringing to 301 the total number of N.S.W. express locos of the ten-wheel arrangement.

Trial run of 3626, an early member of the C36 express type.

Impressive in appearance and of improving performance, the C36 locomotives originally had arched top boilers which gave them a hog-like shape and soon earned them the affectionate nickname of "pigs". The first 10 were built by Eveleigh Workshops and the remaining 65 came from Clyde Engineering. Large turret tenders were fitted to enhance relay working.

As with the C35s, handling a "pig" was not always easy and the long and narrow sloping firebox grate tested the skill of many a sweating engineman. The C36 took over all major express trains until the coming of the C38 Pacifics in the mid-1940s. Belpaire boilers and improved cabs were fitted in later years from 1953.

These extremely versatile machines finished their days on stopping passenger trains and freights of all

The C36 as equipped with a Belpaire firebox and improved cab.

types. One member, No. 3616, became the only locomotive in Australia to be equipped with a Giesl Oblong Ejector, notable for its weirdly "squashed" funnel. The class was scrapped during the 1960s, although three, Nos 3609, 3616 and 3642, were sent to the Rail Transport Museum, Thirlmere.

The C36 design was also adopted by the Commonwealth in 1938 for new express power on the Trans-Australian line between Port Pirie and Kalgoorlie.

Principal dimensions

Driving wheels	5 ft 9 in	1753 mm
Cylinders	23 × 26 in	584 × 660 mm
Pressure	180 lb	1241 kPa
Weight	159 tons	161.5 tonnes
Tractive effort	30,500 lb	13 835 kg

Built 1925

1903–1928   C30T Class   4-6-0

Electrification of the Sydney suburban system in the late 1920s meant loss of employment for a large number of C30-class tank locomotives. With considerable running life ahead, an opportunity was taken to rebuild 77 to a light tender design to replace ageing motive power on country branches. As converted, the locos became known as the somewhat confusing "C30T". Side tanks and bunker were removed and the trailing bogie was taken off to give a 4-6-0 arrangement; tenders of varying capacities came from obsolete locomotives.

Converted from suburban tank, the C30T was assigned to light-line duties in the 1930s.

The C30T worked successfully and greatly improved the passenger, freight and mixed operations on many lightly ballasted country branches. Almost half of the converted locos were later fitted with new boilers and superheaters.

They were eventually replaced by the lower horsepower diesels and scrapped as boiler replacements or major overhauls became due. Those preserved include No. 3001 at Thirlmere; 3028 and 3090 at the Hunter Valley Steam Museum; 3026 at Parkes; 3075 at Cowra, and 3016 and 3102 at Canberra.

Principal dimensions

Driving wheels	4 ft 7 in	1397 mm
Cylinders	19 × 24 in	483 × 610 mm
Pressure	160 lb	1103 kPa
Weight	85 tons	86.4 tonnes
Tractive effort	21,000 lb	9525 kg

Built 1928–33

1943 C38 Class 4-6-2

Under the leadership of Harold Young, last of the N.S.W.R.'s truly "steam" Chief Mechanical Engineers, the first of the department's Pacific type appeared—locomotives considered by many to be the epitome of the nation's steam motive-power development. The initial five locos were delivered under wartime conditions by Clyde Engineering Co. between 1943 and 1945. Painted a full austerity shade, they were soon dubbed "grey nurse" after the notorious man-eating sharks of the N.S.W. coast. A further batch of 25 locos followed from the Locomotive Workshops at Eveleigh (13) and Cardiff, near Newcastle (12). Though the first five were fitted with a streamlined casing along the boiler top and a distinctive bullet nose with centrally positioned headlight, the follow-on engines were unstreamlined, and in neither shape did the performance of the Pacific appear to be affected in any way.

During the design phase, which began some years before actual construction, consideration was given to providing the new class with up to four cylinders or, more likely, three—as with the V.R.'s S class; finally the two-cylinder principle won selection. However, as built, the weight increased for the first time in

Express power at its peak—streamlined 3801, class leader of the crack Pacific type.

N.S.W.R. passenger fleet beyond 203 tonnes (200 tons) and individual driving axle load increased to a new maximum of 23 tonnes (22 tons 12 cwt), a factor which was to severely limit their radius of operation.

As a Pacific type, the new loco was also the N.S.W.R.'s first, after the long line of ten-wheelers, to have a wide-grate firebox which spread beyond the confines of the frames. Unlike some other big-wheel passenger types, the C38 was not equipped with automatic stoker, yet it seems that feeding the 4.4-m^2 (47 sq ft) grate at high speed remained within the physical capacity of the fireman. Among the novel passenger-engine features introduced with the C38 were one-piece cast steel frames which also incorporated integral cylinders, Boxpok driving wheels, combustion chamber extension of the firebox and the highest boiler pressure in Australia, 1689 kPa (245 lb psi).

The C38 became the engine of the Melbourne Limited, the Riverina and all other major trains of the Southern line; it also ran other crack passenger trains such as the Newcastle Flyer and the Central West Express but, except for experimental trials, did not venture on the North Coast line to Brisbane—an example of axle-load limitations. Capable of high

No. 3830: final member of the C38 class, of which only five were streamlined.

speed (although the driving-wheel diameter remained a traditional 1753 mm or 5 ft 9 in), the Pacifics kept to 113-km/h (70-mph) schedules on the often steeply graded and curving main lines, yet in excess of 129 km/h (80 mph) has been recorded. With dieselization the class was assigned to second-level passenger running and increasingly to the freight roster. Three C38s have been preserved at Thirlmere: the class leader 3801 (streamlined), 3820, and the last member, 3830, which is held for the Museum of Applied Arts and Sciences. In 1970 No. 3801 was the first and so far the only steam loco in Australia to travel across the continent on the new standard-gauge link from Sydney to Perth, a distance of some 3960 km (2461 miles).

Principal dimensions

Driving wheels	5 ft 9 in	1753 mm
Cylinders	$21\frac{1}{2} \times 26$ in	546×660 mm
Pressure	245 lb	1689 kPa
Weight	195 tons	198.1 tonnes
streamlined	201 tons	204.2 tonnes
Tractive effort	36,200 lb	16 420 kg

Built 1943–9

GOODS TYPE

1865   E17 Class   0-6-0

With the Great Southern line reaching the foothills of the Southern Highlands at Picton by 1863, the Railway Department could see a need for more powerful and reliable engines to handle goods trains over the steep grades under construction to Mittagong and beyond. Adopting a long boiler design which had been proved in the United Kingdom, orders were placed with Robert Stephenson & Co. for nine locomotives, which entered service between 1865 and 1867.

Oldest freight engine in N.S.W., No. 18 is an 1865 Robert Stephenson 0-6-0.

Subsequent orders went to Stephenson for six more which were erected locally by Mort & Co. in 1870–1. Another local builder, Vale & Lacey, was successful in obtaining a contract for a further six, which were issued to traffic between 1870 and 1873. Robert Stephenson delivered a further two locomotives of the class to replace those destroyed in the Emu Plains accident of 1878.

The E17s were withdrawn after about 30 years' running, several being sold in working condition to coal mines within the State. After almost 100 years in government and colliery duty No. 18 was acquired by the Rail Transport Museum, and can be seen at Thirlmere, where it is the oldest engine in the R.T.M.'s possession.

Principal dimensions
Driving wheels	4 ft 0 in	1219 mm
Cylinders	18 × 24 in	457 × 610 mm
Pressure	120 lb	827 kPa
Weight	50½ tons	51.3 tonnes
Tractive effort	15,600 lb	7076 kg

Built 1865–79

1877 Z19 Class 0-6-0

When the colony's rail lines reached out almost to the borders, another urgent need for motive power arose,

Delivered by Beyer, Peacock in 1877, the 0-6-0 Z19 outlasted most other N.S.W.R. steam locos.

particularly for goods operations. Orders were placed with Beyer, Peacock & Co. for 50 locomotives based on the E17 class 0-6-0 long-boiler design of 1865. Eventually the number grew to 77 from Beyer, Peacock and a local builder, Henry Vale. Certain modifications were introduced from 1891 to improve the usefulness of the 0-6-0s as they took up a variety of duties all over the State. A 40-km/h (25-mph) speed limit was imposed because of the rigid wheelbase and they were then concentrated on shunting and light branch lines. Fourteen were also rebuilt as 2-6-4 tank locomotives and a number were sold for industrial and colliery use. No. 1905, first loco to cross the Sydney Harbour Bridge, has been retained at the Rail Transport Museum, Thirlmere. Nos 1904 and 1923 are stored at the Hunter Valley Rail Museum, while No. 1919 is at Forbes.

Principal dimensions
Driving wheels	4 ft 0 in	1219 mm
Cylinders	18 × 24 in	457 × 610 mm
Pressure	150 lb	1034 kPa
Weight	60¼ tons	61.2 tonnes
Tractive effort	19,450 lb	8822 kg

Built 1877–86

1879 Z28/Z29 Class 2-8-0

Baldwin Locomotive Works supplied the first Consolidation freight locomotives on the N.S.W. system—11 in all—in 1879.

These were then the most powerful engines in Australia and, in a sense, the forerunners of the standard goods design that was to follow 17 years later. Conforming to a typical American outline of the day, they were fitted with canister steam and sand domes, balloon stacks and large wooden cabs. An

The Baldwin J(483) class were first N.S.W.R. locos to exceed 100 tonnes (101.6 tons) weight.

additional 20 engines of similar but larger design, of which two were compounds, were supplied by the same builder in 1891 for goods working over the Blue Mountains, while a further four 2-8-0s were completed by Eveleigh Workshops; all 35 were later grouped as the J class and remained in freight working until dislodged by the more modern D50s and D53s. They were scrapped during the 1930s, and unfortunately no examples of these impressive-looking locomotives have survived.

Principal dimensions

Driving wheels	4 ft 3 in	1295 mm
Cylinders	22 × 26 in	559 × 660 mm
Pressure	140 lb	965 kPa
Weight	100 tons	101.6 tonnes
Tractive effort	29,000 lb	13 154 kg

Built 1879–96

1882　Z25 Class　2-6-0

Designed with a leading pony truck for negotiating sharp curves, these Moguls (2-6-0s) were a follow-on to the successful 0-6-0 goods type introduced in 1877.

Later shape of the Z25 introduced in 1881 as the first Mogul (2-6-0) on the N.S.W.R.

Beyer, Peacock delivered them in varying batches between 1881 and 1885, and at the time they were considered to be ahead of contemporary design for this type of motive power. Highly successful in goods and "push-up" working, their low-wheel performance was improved after reboilering in 1911. Some continued a busy working life, mainly on country branches, until the 1960s. Several were sold to collieries and blue-metal quarries; No. 2510 has been preserved at the Rail Transport Museum, Thirlmere; Hunter Valley Steam Rail Museum has No. 2535.

Principal dimensions

Driving wheels	4 ft 0 in	1219 mm
Cylinders	18 × 26 in	457 × 660 mm
Pressure	140 lb	965 kPa
Weight	71½ tons	72.6 tonnes
Tractive effort	19,400 lb	8800 kg

Built 1882–5

1891   Z24 Class   2-6-0

The 25 engines in this class were built by Dubs & Co. in 1891 to augment a batch of similar locomotives in goods working. On arrival they were painted black, in contrast to the green livery of locomotives then in use, and received the nickname of the "Black Moguls".

A 24-class survivor, No. 2414 went to Bunnerong Powerhouse.

They were not impressive as built, but when fitted with Belpaire boilers after 1903 became quite useful on country goods trains and, as the years went by, on light branch tracks. Some were sold and others scrapped as boiler certificates expired. No. 2419 is at Thirlmere; 2408 and 2414 have been preserved by the Hunter Valley Rail Museum; 2413 is at Canberra.

Principal dimensions

Driving wheels	4 ft 0 in	1219 mm
Cylinders	18 × 26 in	457 × 660 mm
Pressure	140 lb	965 kPa
Weight	76¼ tons	77.5 tonnes
Tractive effort	19,400 lb	8800 kg

Built 1891

1896 D50/D53/D55 Classes 2-8-0

The first five of a new "Australian Consolidation" freight locomotive design delivered to the N.S.W. Railways in the late 1890s were destined to be the leaders of the most plentiful class on the system plus two very similar derivative classes—in all a total of 590 engines, surely a numerical reputation that is hard to match. Intended for freight trains, the D50 class proved very reliable. Under the direction of W. Thow, Chief Mechanical Engineer, 290 were built up to 1912. They were equipped with Belpaire boilers and Thow's favourite Allan straight-link valve gear; most were superheated from 1912; all had the familiar Thow "porthole" cab. Five builders contributed to the original class—Beyer, Peacock (151), Dubs & Co. (5), Neilson Reid & Co. (10), North British Locomotive Co. (84) and Clyde Engineering Co. (30).

Follow-on to the original D50s, the consolidation D53 first appeared in 1912.

In 1912, Clyde Engineering delivered the first of the D53 class, which were virtually identical to the earlier locos except for larger fireboxes, flanges on all driving wheels, and superheaters. Eventually 190 were supplied, 160 by Clyde and 30 from Eveleigh Workshops.

The basic design features of the D50/D53 classes were retained for the D55 built between 1918 and 1925, except that the 120 in this class were fitted with the unusual Southern valve gear. All were constructed by Clyde Engineering; 70 of the D55 class were fitted to burn oil during the coal shortage of the late 1940s.

The 55 standard goods displaying Southern valve gear—and original number.

Virtually all 590 members of the three derivative classes were withdrawn and scrapped as boiler replacements and major overhauls became due and dieselization advanced. Three have been preserved at the Thirlmere Museum. These are D50 class 5096, D53 class 5461 and D55 class 5595.

Hunter Valley Rail Museum has acquired Nos 5069, 5132 and 5353, while 5367 was sent to a depot at Cowra. Another loco, 5112, known as "Ben Chifley's engine", has been preserved in Bathurst where the former engine driver-Prime Minister lived and worked.

Principal dimensions

Driving wheels	4 ft 3 in	1295 mm
Cylinders	22 × 26 in	559 × 660 mm
(D50)	21 × 26 in	533 × 660 mm
Pressure	160 lb	1103 kPa
Weight (D50)	107 tons	108.7 tonnes
(D53)	135 tons	137.2 tonnes
(D55)	127 tons	129 tonnes
Tractive effort (D50)	28,800 lb	13 063 kg
(D53)	33,600 lb	15 241 kg
(D55)	33,600 lb	15 241 kg

Built 1896–1925

1913 Z27 Class 2-6-0

Built by the Hunslet Engine Co., these eight small but useful English-style locos were delivered to the Public Works Department for rail construction trains in 1913. Four years later the N.S.W. Railways took over as constructing authority and acquired the Hunslet

With N.S.W. cowcatcher, 27-class 2708 came from the Public Works Department.

machines as well as several other nondescript types. Although designed for rough work, the locomotives were well equipped with Belpaire boilers and Walschaert valve gear with flat D valves in steam chests above the cylinders. The N.S.W.R. assigned them to light branches, although problems existed on sharp curves. Eventually all were stationed at Narrabri West for operation on the North-West branches. They retained the distinctive cut-away cabs and cowcatchers, although larger tenders were fitted between 1929 and 1938. No. 2705 was retained for vintage train working and is on display at the Rail Transport Museum, Thirlmere.

Principal dimensions

Driving wheels	4 ft 0 in	1219 mm
Cylinders	18 × 24 in	457 × 610 mm
Pressure	160 lb	1103 kPa
Weight	93 tons	94.5 tonnes
Tractive effort	19,200 lb	8709 kg

Built 1913

1929　D57 Class/D58 Class (1950)　4-8-2

Massive in every sense, the first Mountain type appeared on N.S.W. rails in 1929, at the culmination of E. E. Lucy's reign as Chief Mechanical Engineer. The locomotives were also the first to have three simple cylinders—those outside controlled by Walschaert valve gear, and the inside by Gresley conjugating gear. Other "firsts" were a single-piece cast-steel frame, a cast-steel frame for the trailing truck, power reverse gear and mechanical stoker. Classed D57, they took over the heavy freights on the steeply graded sections of the Mountains, South, and Illawarra lines, except that the 22.4-tonne (22-ton) axle load of their large tenders prevented their use beyond Wallerawang,

Largest N.S.W.R. non-articulated freights, the Mountain-class D57 of 1929.

Sister class of the D57, the 4-8-2 heavy-freight D58s appeared in 1950.

Junee and Thirroul respectively. They were banned from the North line owing to low bridge capacities.

The 25 members of the class were supplied by Clyde Engineering with tenders built at Mort's Dock. The D57 class also performed quite successfully in occasional tests hauling top link passenger trains including the Melbourne Limited.

In 1950 the first of an "improved" version of the D57 emerged from Eveleigh Workshops—the D58 class, which varied only in a minor reduction in cylinder diameter and the use of a toothed quadrant and rack drive on the inside cylinder valve gear. Of the proposed order for 25 locomotives, only 13 were completed, 11 from Eveleigh and two by Cardiff Shops. Work was then suspended owing to lack of funds, and was never resumed because of the adoption of diesel power. Of the two classes, only one representative has been retained: No. 5711 at Thirlmere.

Principal dimensions

Driving wheels	5 ft 0 in	1524 mm
Cylinders	23¼ × 28 in	591 × 711 mm
Pressure	200 lb	1379 kPa
Weight	228 tons	231.6 tonnes
Tractive effort	56,000 lb	25 401 kg

Built 1929–30

1952   D59 Class   2-8-2

Even at the debut of the diesel programme, steam motive-power shortages continued to plague the railways as they had almost 90 years earlier. On this final occasion the N.S.W.R. turned to America and ordered 20 light Mikados (2-8-2s) from Baldwin-Lima-Hamilton to the pattern of the U.S. Government's War Department design. Delays occurred through the Department specifying a shorter tender so that the locos could fit on 18.3-m (60-ft) turntables, and the class was not delivered until 1952–3 at the same time as the first main-line diesels arrived.

The D59s, which as a type had seen war and American Marshall Aid service in many corners of the globe, were found to be equally useful alongside the Pigs and Standard Goods. Known for a typical "modern Yankee" appearance and a booming steamboat whistle, they were first assigned to the coal traffic between Newcastle and Sydney and later worked

The 2-8-2 D59, a World War II design from Baldwin-Lima-Hamilton Corp.

extensively in the north and south. Delivered as oil burners, they were converted to coal fuel. Withdrawals began in 1969. Those retained are Nos 5908 and 5910 at Thirlmere and 5917 by a private owner; Hunter Valley Railway Museum has also acquired 5920. Nos 5910 and 5917 are in operating condition.

Principal dimensions

Driving wheels	5 ft 0 in	1524 mm
Cylinders	21 × 28 in	533 × 711 mm
Pressure	200 lb	1379 kPa
Weight	151 tons	153.4 tonnes
Tractive effort	35,000 lb	15 876 kg

Built 1952–3

1952 AD60 Class 4-8-4 + 4-8-4

Although other Australian systems had operated Garratt-type locomotives, the first Beyer Garratts on the N.S.W. system were also to be Australia's largest and most powerful steam locos. In fact, with a weight

Largest articulated loco in Australia, the 60-class Beyer Garratt.

approaching 269 tonnes (265 tons) and an overall length of 32.9 m (108 ft) they were among the largest Garratts ever operated in the world. Also, they were the first Beyer Garratts to be provided with cast-steel engine frames and integrally cast cylinders. Though the original intention was to acquire 50 of these articulated mammoths, the Department sought to have part of the contract cancelled owing to a shortage of funds. Eventually 42 completed units were acquired from Beyer, Peacock, and the unassembled parts for the remainder were also purchased as "spares".

Intended for coal haulage over the Blue Mountains, they were soon placed on the heavy freight roster over most of the system; a light axle load (despite their huge weight) suited them for wheat, concentrates and general traffic on most normal outback lines. Numerous modifications were carried out to make the Garratts more adaptable and to satisfy enginemen's requirements. The decline of the class began as early as 1955 when the introduction of diesel power rendered some superfluous soon after assembly; however a number lingered in useful service until 1970. No. 6040 has been preserved at Thirlmere; 6042 is at a Cowra depot and 6039 at Hunter Valley Rail Museum, while 6029 is at Canberra.

Principal dimensions

Driving wheels	4 ft 7 in	1397 mm
Cylinders	19¼ × 26 in	489 × 660 mm
Pressure	200 lb	1379 kPa
Weight	264 tons	268.2 tonnes
Tractive effort	63,000 lb	28 576 kg

Built 1952–7

TANK AND MISCELLANEOUS TYPES

1879　X10 Class　0-4-0T

The Railway Department acquired a substantial number of crane locomotives of varying size, beginning with three of 4.1-tonne (4-ton) capacity ordered from Dubs & Co. in 1879. Of conventional design, these were side tanks with minimal protection for the crew. The crane, fitted on top of the boiler, was mainly used in lifting locomotive parts, rubbish kibbles and any other heavy item that required transport in and around locomotive depots, workshops and station yards. One of the Dubs cranes, No. 1034, is on exhibition at the Rail Transport Museum at Thirlmere.

An 0-4-0T side tank luffing crane loco, No. 1052, built by Hawthorn Leslie in 1914, has been preserved by the Hunter Valley Steam Rail Museum.

Crane loco 1052, now at Hunter Valley Museum.

Principal dimensions

Driving wheels	3 ft 1 in	940 mm
Cylinders	10 × 20 in	254 × 508 mm
Pressure	140 lb	965 kPa
Weight	30 tons	30.5 tonnes
Tractive effort	6000 lb	2722 kg

Built 1879

1884 Z18 Class 0-6-0T

Six small locomotives were built by Vulcan Foundry for suburban trains in Sydney. Their low driving wheels made them more suited to shunting duties, to which they were later transferred at Sydney station and in various locomotive depots; some were fitted with cranes. Two were sold to colliery companies and one was used extensively on the Public Works Department lines at Port Kembla for many years. No. 1803 is on display at the Rail Transport Museum, Thirlmere.

Insufficient speed relegated the 18-class 0-6-0Ts to shunting duties.

Principal dimensions

Driving wheels	4 ft 0 in	1219 mm
Cylinders	15 × 22 in	381 × 559 mm
Pressure	140 lb	965 kPa
Weight	34 tons	34.5 tonnes
Tractive effort	11,550 lb	5239 kg

Built 1884

1885   X10 Class   2-4-0T

To provide faster motive power for suburban operations, Beyer, Peacock was requested to build 12 small tank locomotives with large driving wheels. These entered service in 1885–6 and were followed by a further six from Henry Vale of Sydney in 1887. Though well regarded and reliable, they were withdrawn from passenger trains after an accident involving one of the class at Sydenham in 1901. All were transferred to depot duties, with a number later being sold to colliery

The short-lived 2-4-0 suburban tank, 1033 of old class F351.

and industrial users. By the late 1960s all had been withdrawn; No. 1033 is on display at Thirlmere, and No. 1042 has been preserved at Cardiff Workshops.

Principal dimensions

Driving wheels	5 ft 1 in	1549 mm
Cylinders	15 × 22 in	381 × 559 mm
Pressure	140 lb	965 kPa
Weight	38½ tons	39.1 tonnes
Tractive effort	9100 lb	4128 kg

Built 1885–7

1891 Z20 Class 2-6-4T

Imported initially to handle short-distance coal trains around Newcastle, these smart little locomotives achieved their greatest usefulness on passenger trains. The first 12 delivered by Beyer, Peacock in 1891 had many of their parts interchangeable with those of the 0-6-0 A93 goods locomotives introduced in 1877, and in the early 1900s 21 of the 0-6-0s were also converted

A conglomerate, the Z20 class were intended for coal working.

to tank design. Belpaire boilers were fitted in 1906–7.

After being displaced from coal haulage by more powerful locomotives, the tanks were used for shunting and suburban goods trains until transferred to the passenger roster on such short, light lines as Richmond–Kurrajong, Campbelltown–Camden, Morpeth and Parramatta–Rogans Hill.

Some were sold to colliery operators, while others continued their useful life shunting at Port Kembla; all had been withdrawn by 1970.

No. 2029 is on exhibition at the Rail Transport Museum, Thirlmere.

Principal dimensions
Driving wheels	4 ft 0 in	1219 mm
Cylinders	18 × 24 in	457 × 610 mm
Pressure	150 lb	1034 kPa
Weight	61½ tons	62.5 tonnes
Tractive effort	19,400 lb	8800 kg

Built 1891–1911

1892 Z26 Class 2-6-2ST

To handle coal and mineral trains on the steeply graded Illawarra line, these saddle tanks—unusual machines for N.S.W.—spent most of their career as shunters around the freight and passenger terminals.

The Z26 saddle tank, introduced on mineral trains in the 1890s.

Twenty in number, the class was built by Dubs & Co. and delivered in 1892. Though first used on the coal and blue metal trains, they were also pressed into service on holiday-excursion specials; the large capacity of the saddle tanks made them ideal for such passenger working when water supplies were restricted along the route. A number were also stationed at Eskbank, Lithgow, for colliery and industrial haulage.

Replaced on the main lines by larger locomotives, they assumed more mundane shunting and push-up duties and could be observed at most important terminals and depots until 1970.

No. 2606 is displayed at Thirlmere. No. 2605 is stored by the Commonwealth Portland Cement Company at Portland on the Mudgee line.

Principal dimensions
Driving wheels	4 ft 0 in	1219 mm
Cylinders	18 × 26 in	457 × 660 mm
Pressure	150 lb	1034 kPa
Weight	66 tons	67.1 tonnes
Tractive effort	20,800 lb	9435 kg

Built 1892

1896 Z13 Class 4-4-2T

Between 1896 and 1902 20 locomotives were converted from the C79 passenger 4-4-0 type by extension of the frame to accommodate a coal bunker and water tank. A trailing axle was added as well as side tanks; 18 of the

Before electrification, the CC79 tanks worked Sydney suburban services. Later they were classed Z13.

class received Belpaire fireboxes. After the more powerful S-class tank displaced them from Sydney suburban running, they were sent to light-line branches such as the Yass Tramway and Picton–Mittagong, and also ran small passenger trains in the Casino district of the far north coast. Two have been retained at the Rail Transport Museum: No. 1301, the class leader, now 100 years old (as originally built)—the oldest serviceable locomotive at Thirlmere; and No. 1307.

Principal dimensions

Driving wheels	5 ft 6 in	1676 mm
Cylinders	18 × 24 in	457 × 610 mm
Pressure	140 lb	965 kPa
Weight	52 tons	52.8 tonnes
Tractive effort	13,100 lb	5942 kg

Built 1896–1902

1903   C30 Class   4-6-4T

Sydney's burgeoning suburban traffic at the turn of the century required more powerful locomotives, particularly on the steeply graded Main North, North Shore and Illawarra lines. The resultant 4-6-4T is considered to be one of the most successful suburban tank designs of its time in the world. Beyer, Peacock supplied the first batch, which were placed in service between 1903 and 1905. Eventually the class grew to number 145, deliveries coming again from Beyer, Peacock, and from Eveleigh Workshops. Highly successful and extremely versatile, the C30s were used extensively in Sydney and Newcastle; they were also rostered to work the Cessnock Express between Broadmeadow and Cessnock.

Electrification of the Sydney suburban system rendered the large class superfluous; as they were too valuable to scrap, more than 70 were converted to a

The C30 tank, a mainstay of Sydney services in the steam suburban days.

light tender design (see C30T Class, p. 66). The remaining tanks stayed in service on outer-suburban and Newcastle passenger trains and were also used on short country branches as well as for selected banking duties and car shunting at major terminals. They were finally withdrawn during the 1950s and 1960s. Several are preserved: Nos 3137 and 3085 at Thirlmere; 3046 by the Hunter Valley Rail Museum; 3112 at a Cowra depot.

Principal dimensions

Driving wheels	4 ft 7 in	1397 mm
Cylinders	19 × 24 in	483 × 610 mm
Pressure	160 lb	1103 kPa
Weight	72 tons	73.2 tonnes
Tractive effort	20,160 lb	9144 kg

Built 1903–17

1916 X10 Class 0-4-0T

Five of these diminutive Manning Wardle saddle tanks were imported in 1916 by the Public Works Department for railway construction. They were transferred to the control of the N.S.W.R. in 1917. Four were later sold, the one retained later being numbered 1021. After

No. 1021 of the X10 class began working on North Coast construction trains.

construction tasks were completed, the little locomotive, often known as the "Baby Singer", was used as a shunter at Cardiff Workshops (near Newcastle) for many years. Later it was employed as a steam-raising plant at Enfield Locomotive Depot and also as a shunter. It has been retained as a static display at the Rail Transport Museum.

Principal dimensions

Driving wheels	3 ft 0 in	914 mm
Cylinders	12 × 18 in	305 × 457 mm
Pressure	160 lb	1103 kPa
Weight	21 tons	21.3 tonnes
Tractive effort	9,200 lb	4173 kg

Built 1916

1916 X10 Class 0-4-0ST

Two small saddle-tank locomotives built for the Public Works Department by Vulcan Iron Works of U.S.A.

came into the possession of the Railway Department in 1916. They were used on railway construction duties before retiring to shunting at Enfield Depot. During World War II they were also hired by the U.S. Army for use in Army Stores areas near Parramatta.

Though withdrawn from service in 1964–70, No. 1022 still operates on the Parramatta Park Steam Tramway.

Saddle tanks were rare in N.S.W. No. 1022 was handed down from the P.W.D.

Principal dimensions

Driving wheels	3 ft 0 in	914 mm
Cylinders	12 × 18 in	305 × 457 mm
Pressure	150 lb	1034 kPa
Weight	27 tons	27.4 tonnes
Tractive effort	8,640 lb	3919 kg

Built 1916

1879 Steam Tram Motor 0-4-0

Steam tram motors were introduced to Sydney in 1879 for the opening of the Elizabeth Street line from Bridge Street to the Railway. Built to a standard enclosed design introduced by Baldwin Locomotive Works, the fleet grew to a total of 121, of which Baldwin itself supplied 100; the others were made locally either by contractors or in the Tramway workshops.

Within 15 years steam tram services had spread over most of the inner southern, eastern and western suburbs. Isolated systems were opened in Newcastle, Maitland, Broken Hill and around the Sydney area in Kogarah, Manly, Arncliffe, Sutherland and Parramatta. A privately owned steam tramway existed in Parramatta for over 60 years.

Several country rail branches were also worked with these dinky locos in those years when the Railways

Baldwin motor 38—the 0-4-0 wheels hidden from passing horse traffic.

Department controlled the tramways. Electric traction nudged steam off the streets, although some government steam tramways continued until 1937. Two motors have been retained; the class leader No. 1, which is stored (for eventual display, it is hoped) by the Museum of Applied Arts and Sciences, Sydney, and No. 103 which operates at Parramatta Park.

Principal dimensions

Driving wheels	3 ft 0 in	914 mm
Cylinders	11 × 16 in	279 × 406 mm
Pressure	130 lb	896 kPa
Weight	14 tons	14.2 tonnes
Tractive effort	5,700 lb	2585 kg

Built 1879–1923

Locos never built: artist's impression of the N.S.W.R.'s ambitious 2-6-8-0 Mallett.

AUSTRALIAN NATIONAL RAILWAYS COMMISSION

The Australian National Railways Commission (A.N.R.) was established in 1975 to take over the function of the Commonwealth Railways and to be the Federal Government's instrumentality to operate those rail systems which might be purchased from any of the States. Since its formation, in addition to the C.R., the A.N.R. now incorporates the former Tasmanian Government Railways and the non-metropolitan lines of South Australia.

The Commonwealth Railways began operation in October 1917 with the running of the first Trans-Australian express from Port Augusta to Kalgoorlie. The North and Central Australia railways were added to the C.R. in 1918–26. A.N.R. routes now stretch from Kalgoorlie to Cockburn on the S.A.–N.S.W.

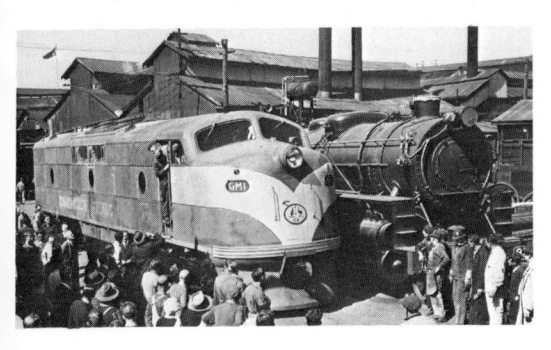

Precursor of A.N.R.'s diesels, GM1 alongside 2-8-2 L class, at Clyde, 1952.

border and (apart from the Adelaide network which remains part of a State Transport Authority) to Mt Gambier in the south and Serviceton on the Victorian border; as well, it has the isolated Eyre Peninsula division. In the far south it operates between Burnie, Launceston and Hobart. Across the broad, standard and narrow gauges, trackage totals 8511 km (5288 miles) with more than 14,000 pieces of rolling stock.

The North Australia Railway has been closed and "moth-balled", but north-east from Tarcoola on the T.A.R. a new heavy-duty standard-gauge line of 831 km (516 miles) is being built towards Alice Springs. By 1981 it will replace the flood-prone narrow gauge track that, dating from 1878, was part of a grand plan for the north-south transcontinental railway.

As a post-dieselization entity, the A.N.R. has never operated a steam locomotive in regular traffic (it presently has some 2,300 diesels), yet its member systems grew up on the iron horse.

Incidentally one should note that the former S.A.R. broad-gauge steam locomotives retained for enthusiast excursions out of Adelaide are owned, at the time of writing, not by A.N.R., but by the S.A. State Transport Authority (S.A.S.T.A.-Metrorail), which has the responsibility for running commuter trains in the immediate Adelaide suburban area. The locos Rx 207 and 224, 520 and 621 are usually operated by S.A.S.T.A. in conjunction with the S.A. Branch of the Australian Railway Historical Society.

AUSTRALIAN NATIONAL RAILWAYS
1. Central Region
(Ex-South Australian Railways)
1856

South Australia alone contains all three government gauges within its limits—broad, standard and narrow; a very dubious thing to boast about, one might add. Beginning as broad gauge, the first line (for which the great Isambard Kingdom Brunel was consulting engineer) opened between North Terrace, Adelaide, and Port Adelaide dock, 12 km (7 miles), on 21 April 1856. The narrow gauge was inaugurated far to the north, between Port Augusta and Quorn, in 1879. Having thrown uniformity to the winds, the 1067-mm (3 ft 6 in) rails continued to forge northwards towards Oodnadatta and eastwards to Broken Hill, and to

Wild West Baldwins at the Quorn-Port Augusta opening in 1882.

radiate in the Mt Gambier south-east pocket and on the Eyre Peninsula. Meanwhile, broad gauge came up to meet the narrow gauge at Terowie, to spread into the Murray lands and, on 19 January 1887, joining at Serviceton with the V.R. western line from Melbourne.

The observer of South Australia's locomotive development will be struck by the enormous gulf that existed between the pre-1920 broad-gauge engines—small, low-powered, colonial-style machines that had changed little in, say, 40 years— and the great steam goliaths that were suddenly to erupt on the scene as Commissioner Webb's "Americanization" took hold. The crowds that gathered on a Port Adelaide dock in 1926 to gaze wonderingly at a group of locomotives might well have been excused for asking themselves if the ship that carried them had been diverted from its rightful destination—the U.S.A. The new machines were massive Mountain, Pacific and Mikado types, designs of Chief Mechanical Engineer F. Shea, and built in Newcastle-on-Tyne, England, at the works of Sir William Armstrong Whitworth & Co. The days of three veteran Rx class struggling up Mt Lofty with the Melbourne Express were almost at an end!

In a matter of weeks the new engines were assembled, tested and put to work—the 500 Mountains and the 600 Pacifics between them were desitned to share all heavy haulage on the main line to Victoria. The ten 600-class Pacifics rode on 1905-mm (6 ft 3 in) driving wheels, the tallest ever used on a modern Australian locomotive—only the 1981-mm (6 ft 6 in) wheels of South Australia's 1894 four-coupled S class were larger. The 500 class dwarfed any loco yet seen on broad gauge, with tractive effort of 23 133 kg (51,000 lb), later raised to 26 762 kg (59,000 lb) and measuring 25.6 m (84 ft) overall; until then no existing S.A.R. goods engine had produced an effort of more than 9977 kg (22,000 lb). Third locomotive of the group was the 700 class, an 18 325-kg (40,400-lb) tractive effort Mikado intended to serve on the State's lighter lines.

From experience gained with its 1926 imports, South Australian Railways went on to design other gallant engines, all of them built at Islington Workshops—the 620 light-line Pacifics, the 710 follow-on Mikados and the mammoth 720 class of 1938, with booster achieving 23 587-kg (52,000-lb) tractive effort, the only Australian loco to have the Berkshire (2-8-4) wheel arrangement. In 1943 came the classic submarine-shaped 500, a passenger and mixed-traffic 4-8-4 that could work across 27.2-kg (60-lb) rail and, on main lines, comfortably reach 113 km/h (70 mph).

In retrospect one might doubt the efficiency with which the S.A.R. was able to utilize its new engine power, hampered as it was by a mixture of track restrictions, heavy axle loads and traffic growth that did not always match the forecasts. Yet on S.A.R.'s broad gauge, the controversial regime of W. A. Webb, a railwayman imbued with the big-engine traditions of Missouri, Kansas and Texas Railroad—despite considerable overspending that led to his retirement in 1930—brought about an episode in Australian locomotive history that is not easily dismissed.

Gauge 1600 mm (5 ft 3 in)

PASSENGER TYPE

1886–1899   Rx Class   4-6-0

The steeply graded South line from Adelaide presented a continual challenge to the Locomotive Branch. To climb the 1-in-45 slopes in the late 1880s, a ten-wheeler was introduced which would have among its duties the hauling of the Inter-Colonial (Melbourne) Express.

Thirty of the R class were in traffic by 1895, products

Rx 224, one of two ten-wheelers preserved for steam specials.

of Dubs & Co. and James Martin of Gawler. It was soon realized that performance could be improved with a larger boiler, and after conversion the locos were reclassified Rx. Then in 1909 Islington Workshops began issuing the first of a batch of new locomotives built to the improved design and thus known as Rx from the outset.

Generally the class proved quite successful within design limitations—two and sometimes three were needed to haul the Melbourne Express—and by 1916 the 84 in service included the 30 which had been built as Rs.

By 1930 the Webb administration's big engines had displaced the Rx to lesser duties on various sections of the broad gauge; until the 1960s the Rx was still used in strength, mainly for shunting and on short suburban and transfer freights. Several Rx class continued into the 1970s and two have been retained for special excursions: Nos 207 and 224. No. 93 has been preserved at the Mile End Rail Museum, while others can be seen in various country towns as follows: Kapunda (No. 5), Loxton (55), Murray Bridge (160), Victor Harbour (191), Tailem Bend (201), Nuriootpa (217) and Kadina (231).

Principal dimensions

Driving wheels	4 ft 6 in	1372 mm
Cylinders	18 × 24 in	457 × 610 mm
Pressure	175 lb	1207 kPa
Weight	88½ tons	90 tonnes
Tractive effort	21,420 lb	9716 kg

Built 1886–1916

1894 S Class 4-4-0

With a driving-wheel diameter of 1981 mm (6 ft 6 in), the South Australian S class were certainly the high-steppers of the railway scene in the 1890s. These engines had the largest driving wheels ever used on an Australian locomotive and a glimpse of one of the neat, uncluttered eight-wheelers, with flying connecting rods, striding along the flat stretches of the South line to Bordertown was enough to stir the enthusiast's blood.

James Martin & Co. delivered the first 12 in 1894 for passenger work on the more level stretches of the 1600-mm (5 ft 3 in) gauge, and an additional six were in service by 1903. Capable of high speed, the S was assigned to main passenger trains including the Melbourne–Adelaide Express east of Murray Bridge. Among the modifications of later years, the class

S.A.R.'s high-wheel 4-4-0 S class.

received large-capacity bogie tenders which enhanced the appearance even more.

Though demoted by the Webb locos, the S class continued in faithful service for many more years. Scrapping occurred from 1956 on, and though an attempt was made to save one engine, it is unfortunate that none of the elegant high-wheelers was preserved for later generations to admire.

Principal dimensions

Driving wheels	6 ft 6 in	1981 mm
Cylinders	18 × 24 in	457 × 610 mm
Pressure	150 lb	1034 kPa
Weight	61 tons	62 tonnes
Tractive effort	11,812 lb	5358 kg

Built 1894–1903

1926   500 Class   4-8-4

The most powerful of the big engines introduced during the Americanization period, these giants were intended to handle the top passenger trains on the

As landed in 1926, the 500 class with 4-8-2 wheel arrangement.

Rebuilt as booster 4-8-4, the ex-Mountain type later became the 500B.

sharply graded sections of the South line. Despite their obvious American appearance, the 10 in the class were built by Armstrong Whitworth of the U.K. as 4-8-2s; but after 1929 the installation of boosters brought about a replacement of the trailing truck, hence the 4-8-4 wheel arrangement. The 500Bs, as they were properly known, spent virtually all their life handling heavy passenger and freight trains on the South, although they also worked freights northwards to Port Pirie and Terowie. At the time of their delivery, they were the largest locomotives built in the U.K.

A 500 class in silver-and-green livery charging up the grades of the Mount Lofty Range with the stylish wooden sitting and sleeping cars of the Overland is among the fondest memories of steam power at its peak.

The 500 class, ultimately ousted by diesels, were withdrawn between 1958 and 1963; one (504) has been preserved at the Mile End Rail Museum, Adelaide.

Principal dimensions

Driving wheels	5 ft 3 in	1600 mm
Cylinders	26 × 28 in	660 × 711 mm
Pressure	200 lb	1379 kPa
Weight	22 tons	22.4 tonnes
Tractive effort	59,000 lb	26 762 kg

Built 1926

1926   600 Class   4-6-2

As the main "passenger horse" of the Webb motive-power invasion of 1926, these handsome heavy Pacifics were unloaded alongside the mountain-climbing 500s. Almost three times higher in tractive effort than the 4-4-0s, they were also Australia's first 4-6-2s on other than the narrow gauge.

Ten were built by Armstrong Whitworth and entered service on the Overland and other passenger and freight services of the level graded section of the border line to Serviceton. Driving-wheel diameter was the largest of any new Australian loco, although they were restricted to the S.A. maximum of 97 km/h (60 mph).

Limited by a heavy axle load, the 600s were also confined to such lines as Victor Harbour, Terowie and Port Pirie, although they appeared on the Mount Gambier branch after it had been converted from narrow to broad gauge.

They acquired boilers with higher pressures than the original 1379 kPa (200 lb) in the 1930s and classification changed to 600C. Smoke deflectors which did not detract from their racy appearance were added and some received automatic stokers. However the 600 fell

No. 609, Duke of Gloucester, one of the Webb era's heavy Pacifics.

an early victim of the diesel and was among the first of the big power to be scrapped.

All were condemned between 1958 and 1961, and it is regrettable that none was preserved.

Principal dimensions
Driving wheels	6 ft 3 in	1905 mm
Cylinders	24 × 28 in	610 × 711 mm
Pressure	215 lb	1482 kPa
Weight	197 tons	200 tonnes
Tractive effort	39,300 lb	17 826 kg

Built 1926

1936 620 Class 4-6-2

Early in the 1930s the South Australians discovered a distinct gap in their motive-power stable between the "heavies" of the Webb regime and the small power

Sloping smokebox front of the light 620-class Pacific in regular guise.

which had preceded Commissioner Webb's American-style programme. To provide the missing link, a medium-powered but speedy Pacific was put in hand at Islington Workshops in 1936. By 1938 ten of the 620 class were in service, and mainly concentrated on the newly opened direct broad-gauge route to Port Pirie.

With the introduction of the 520s in 1943, the 620s were transferred farther afield, but they continued to give a good account of themselves wherever fast running was required.

For centenary celebrations, 620 class in semi-streamlined guise.

Though essentially small locomotives, they had a well-proportioned appearance and were popular with passengers and crews alike. All were out of service by 1963. One has been retained for enthusiast workings (No. 621), and a fellow class member (No. 624) is on display at Mile End.

Principal dimensions

Driving wheels	5 ft 6 in	1676 mm
Cylinders	18½ × 28 in	470 × 711 mm
Pressure	200 lb	1379 kPa
Weight	140¾ tons	143 tonnes
Tractive effort	25,000 lb	11 340 kg

Built 1936–8

1943 520 Class 4-8-4

Most locomotives built under wartime conditions had an austere or rather more functional appearance—yet this is the last description which could be applied to the dramatic 520 class which were outshopped by Islington in 1943.

Designed specifically for fast running with heavy trains on relatively level track, these locomotives soon achieved a reputation for hard work under difficult

Final development of passenger steam power, South Australia's 520-class 4-8-4.

conditions in all corners of the broad gauge. The "submarine" or "shark-nosed" shape was similar to a design then being introduced on the Pennsylvania Railroad, U.S.A. Eventually 12 were built, and their wheel configuration and weight distribution together with 12-wheel tenders enabled them to operate over both light and heavy track. Capable of non-stop running between Adelaide and Port Pirie, they were fast and efficient steamers. In the post-war coal shortages, they were equipped to burn oil and coal.

Diesels brought a sudden demise to these impressive engines, and within five years from 1961 all had been withdrawn. Fortunately class leader 520 has been retained for enthusiast trains and 523 is preserved at Mile End.

Principal dimensions

Driving wheels	5 ft 6 in	1676 mm
Cylinders	20½ × 28 in	521 × 711 mm
Pressure	215 lb	1482 k Pa
Weight	200½ tons	203.7 tonnes
Tractive effort	32,600 lb	14 787 kg

Built 1943–7

GOODS TYPE

1926   700/710/720 Class   2-8-2/2-8-4

Third of the big-power types introduced by Commissioner Webb was the 700 class, in which the key design feature was an axle load light enough for lines unsuitable to the 500 and 600 classes. Armstrong Whitworth provided the 10 locomotives which were unloaded in 1926. In operation the engines proved so successful that a further 10 with minor modifications were built by Islington in 1928–9 as 710 class.

A larger version with 2-8-4 wheel arrangement and

The light-line 700-class Mikado, another Webb era engine.

Heavy freight 720 class with Australia's only Berkshire wheel arrangement.

booster equipped, known as 720 class, was completed in 1930–43; the four-wheel booster trucks and automatic stokers, in fact, had been intended for conversion of the 600 Pacifics to a 4-6-4 type. Later locos of this powerful 720B type were fitted with 12-wheel tenders.

No. 748 was an UNRRA 2-8-2, originally ordered for China.

Although intended for freight, the 700 and its derivative classes were equally at home on passenger and short suburban trains on the South line. The 700 design was also perpetuated in 20 locomotives which Clyde Engineering Co. built for China under an UNRRA contract after World War II. When the shipment was cancelled due to the fall of the Chinese Nationalist Government, 10 locomotives were sold to the S.A.R., where they became the 740 class; the Commonwealth Railways took the other 10, which remained standard gauge and were designated L class.

The 700 class were renowned for the heavy loads which they handled with ease, maintaining respectable speeds on level and graded track; one (702) has been preserved at the Mile End Rail Museum.

Principal dimensions
Driving wheels   4 ft 9 in   1448 mm
Cylinders   22 × 28 in   559 × 711 mm

Pressure	200 lb	1379 kPa
Weight	171 tons	173.7 tonnes
Tractive effort	40,400 lb	18 325 kg

Built 1926

1951   750 Class   2-8-2

The recurring post-war shortages of motive power, especially for lines of lighter axle loads, coincided with a surplus order of locomotives on the neighbouring Victorian Railways. The S.A.R. availed itself of the opportunity to purchase 10 2-8-2s of the batch which was being delivered by North British of Glasgow, in 1950–1. The design itself was a repeat of the N class of 1925 (see V.R. N class, p. 34), and only minor modifications were required to suit the engines for their new broad-gauge owners. Known as 750s, they were used mainly on the Mallee lines based on Tailem Bend, replacing the smaller Rx class. However, the imports were not popular with S.A.R. enginemen and

The North British 750 class, identical to the V.R.'s parent N class.

the first was withdrawn after only eight years. All were out of service by 1963. Mile End Museum has No. 752.

Principal dimensions

Driving wheels	4 ft 7 in	1397 mm
Cylinders	20 × 26 in	508 × 660 mm
Pressure	175 lb	1207 kPa
Weight	124½ tons	126.5 tonnes
Tractive effort	28,650 lb	12 995 kg

Built 1951

TANK AND MISCELLANEOUS TYPES
1884   P Class   2-4-0T

These tank locomotives with inside cylinders were acquired for suburban passenger working in the Adelaide area. The first six were built by Beyer, Peacock in 1884 and a further 14 were supplied by James Martin of Gawler in 1893. They were used mainly on the Port line and also on the short shuttle service to Mitcham. They also worked to Glenelg before the South Terrace line gave way to an electric

Small suburban tanks, the Adelaide P class.

tramway, and on short services on the Outer Harbour and Semaphore lines.

After shunting duties around Port Adelaide, most of the class remained intact until the late 1950s. No. 117 is on display at the Mile End Rail Museum.

Principal dimensions

Driving wheels	5 ft 0 in	1524 mm
Cylinders	16 × 20 in	406 × 508 mm
Pressure	145 lb	1000 kPa
Weight	33¾ tons	34.2 tonnes
Tractive effort	10,517 lb	4770 kg

Built 1884–93

1902   F Class   4-6-2T

The F-class tanks were introduced to improve on the abilities of the little P class around the Adelaide suburban area. In all, 43 were built—by Islington Shops (21), James Martin (12), and Perry Engineering (10). Affectionately known as "Dollies", the F class were efficient locos capable of spirited running in either direction with reasonably heavy trains. They also

"Dolly Varden" 4-6-2T, as originally introduced for Adelaide working.

served beyond the suburban area and worked to Hamley Bridge, Long Plains and Willunga. Permitted to travel at 97 km/h (60 mph), their crews frequently made the most of the opportunity for fast running; the F also displayed a good acceleration ability, necessary on lines where the stations sometimes were less than a kilometre apart.

The F provided the backbone of the Adelaide suburban system until the introduction of diesel rail cars in the 1950s. Scrapping took place from 1957 onwards. Three have been preserved: No. 255 at Mile End, 251 at Elizabeth and 245 at Gawler North.

Principal dimensions

Driving wheels	5 ft 3 in	1600 mm
Cylinders	$17\frac{1}{2} \times 24$ in	444×610 mm
Pressure	185 lb	1276 kPa
Weight	59 tons	60 tonnes
Tractive effort	18,335 lb	8 317 kg

Built 1902–22

Narrow gauge 1067 mm (3 ft 6 in)

1877   V Class   0-4-4T

South Australia's various narrow-gauge lines were intended ostensibly for horse traction and, in fact, several were worked by this slow plodding form of transport in the early years. As such, the lines were never envisaged to carry heavy loads at anything more than a walking pace, and in these circumstances it is not surprising that the early steam locos provided for such narrow-gauge operations were small in appearance and power.

Consider the eight V-class 0-4-4T tank locomotives first placed in service on the Kingston branch, which

A tiny 0-4-4 V class of 1877 vintage.

until then had been a horse track. Weighing only 15.7 tonnes (15½ tons), these "tiny tots" of the steam brigade were soon relegated to shunting and other minor duties.

The first four were built by Beyer, Peacock and delivered in 1877 and a further four came from the works of James Martin at Gawler in 1893. In later years these locomotives were to be found on other narrow-gauge lines. Several were sold to private users, such as timber companies and the Harbour Board, while two, remarkably, lasted until the early 1950s.

The class leader (9) has been preserved at Naracoorte where it was first in service.

Principal dimensions

Driving wheels	3 ft 0 in	914 mm
Cylinders	9½ × 15 in	241 × 381 mm
Pressure	130 lb	896 kPa
Weight	15½ tons	15.7 tonnes
Tractive effort	4150 lb	1882 kg

Built 1877–93

1878 W Class 2-6-0

For its narrow-gauge lines the S.A.R. of the 1870s acquired quite a stud of light yet reliable 2-6-0 tender locomotives. Classified W, they belonged to a standard design supplied by Beyer, Peacock for colonial operations. The first two were assigned to the Port Pirie–Jamestown line and subsequent deliveries were made from the Manchester foundry between 1878 and 1883, when 36 were in service.

These dependable little locos were allocated to other narrow-gauge lines based on Port Augusta, Naracoorte and Mount Gambier, where they handled all types of trains. Some were sold to rail construction contractors, and a few were eventually returned to the S.A.R. The design was also adopted by the Western Australian Government Railways for engines on the Fremantle–Perth line which opened in 1880. During the early 1900s a classification of Wx was given to 16 of the class which had been rebuilt with larger boilers. In 1911 three W class were acquired by the Commonwealth Government when it assumed control of the North Australia Railway; these were reclassified NF.

Several of the Ws were scrapped during the early 1900s, but most continued to give good service until the late 1920s and a few lasted until 1959.

Narrow gauge wasn't enough: the S.A.R.'s early W class sported a four-wheel tender.

One of the Wx-class rebuilds (No. 18) has been preserved at Naracoorte.

Principal dimensions

Driving wheels	3 ft 3 in	991 mm
Cylinders	12 × 20 in	305 × 508 mm
Pressure	130/145 lb	896/1000 kPa
Weight	30 tons	30.5 tonnes
Tractive effort	7680/8566 lb	3484/3885 kg

Built 1878–83

1885 Y Class 2-6-0

The expansion of narrow-gauge lines in the 1880s called for larger engines than the minimal power then in use. Beyer, Peacock was again consulted and between 1885 and 1890 supplied 48 locomotives of a practical 2-6-0 wheel arrangement, known as Y class.

Further deliveries were made by Islington Workshops (2), and James Martin & Co. (76), until 126 were in operation. Used on all narrow-gauge lines for all types of traffic, they could maintain reasonable schedules despite the small boilers and low wheels. The design was also used on other Australian systems under other classifications (e.g., G class in Western Australia and C in Tasmania). The S.A.R. sold 22 to the Commonwealth Railways in 1941–4, while the Silverton Tramway Co. acquired 21 from Beyer, Peacock for its operations out of Broken Hill to the South Australian border.

Between 1906 and 1924 rebuilds were carried out to 58 of the class, and with larger boilers and Belpaire fireboxes they were reclassified Yx.

The Y and Yx class served the S.A.R. faithfully and several were still operating when narrow-gauge steam was completely withdrawn with gauge standardization of the Broken Hill–Peterborough line in 1970. S.A.R.

"Colonial" outline of the Beyer, Peacock 2-6-0, known as the Y class in S.A.

Y-class 97 and Silverton Tramway Y-class 12 have been preserved at the Mile End Museum; Y82 is preserved at Peterborough, Y141 at Port Lincoln. Two former S.A.R. Y-class locomotives are to be found at the Bassendean Museum, W.A.

Principal dimensions

Driving wheels	3 ft 3 in	991 mm
Cylinders	14 × 20 in	368 × 508 mm
Pressure	145 lb	1000 kPa
Weight	47¾ tons	48.5 tonnes
Tractive effort	13,290 lb	6028 kg

Built 1885–98

1903   T Class   4-8-0

Managing a fully fledged narrow-gauge system would have imposed problems enough for a railway that found itself denied the finance needed for continued development as the years rolled by to the depression age of the 1930s. On the narrow gauge we should note that T. S. Roberts' highly successful T class of 1903 was the one original design to produce a tractive effort in the 9072-kg (20,000-lb) range until the arrival (following a brief spell with the ASGs) of the Franco-Belge Beyer Garratts 50 years later.

As the first "original" design for the narrow gauge, this heavy 12-wheeler also turned out to be one of South Australia's most versatile locomotives. Between 1903 and 1917 a total of 78 T class were built—by Islington Workshops (4), James Martin (34), and Walkers Ltd (40). With substantially improved haulage capacity they virtually took over all major operations on the 1067-mm (3 ft 6 in) system, including the punishing ore traffic and the overnight passenger expresses of the Broken Hill line.

S.A.R.'s own T-class 4-8-0 as it first appeared "ex-Workshops"

The Ts appeared to be quite at ease on freight, passenger and shunting duties. Modifications included a term as oil burners. Versatility was further emphasized by the five converted to broad gauge in 1923 and reclassified Tx; these reverted to the narrow gauge in 1949.

A number worked north with the Commonwealth

Railways during World War II, and six were sold to the Tasmanian Railways. Survivors of the T class were still in use when the Broken Hill line went over to standard gauge in 1970. No. 186 has been retained in serviceable condition for the enthusiast-operated Pichi Richi Railway, and another (No. 251) is at the Bellarine Railway, Queenscliff. No. 253 is preserved at Mile End, 181 is displayed in Broken Hill, 224 at Millicent and 199 at Peterborough.

Principal dimensions

Driving wheels	3 ft 7 in	1092 mm
Cylinders	$16\frac{1}{2} \times 22$ in	419×559 mm
Pressure	185 lb	1276 kPa
Weight	$78\frac{1}{2}$ tons	79.75 tonnes
Tractive effort	21,904 lb	9935 kg

Built 1903–17

1953   400 Class   4-8-2+2-8-4

The 1950s upsurge in ore and freight traffic on the narrow gauge from Broken Hill to Port Pirie found even the existing T class unable to cope. After a pause of some years, the S.A.R. returned to Beyer, Peacock—this time for 10 Garratt locomotives which would provide maximum haulage power consistent with the low axle loading of the 1067-mm (3 ft 6 in) gauge.

Construction was sub-contracted to Beyer, Peacock's associated company in France, Société Franco-Belge, and the locomotives were delivered in 1953. Though built as oil burners they were adaptable for coal firing and could also be converted to standard or broad gauge if the necessity arose. The 400s capably ran the big ore trains but the introduction of diesel-electrics and gauge standardization put them out to grass between 1966 and 1970.

It is recalled that the 400s were not the only Garratts

Société Franco-Belge built Garratt 409 under Beyer licence.

Purchased from the West, ASG 301 went into interim service at Peterborough.

operated by the S.A.R. Six of the ASG design (see p. 121) were purchased from the West in 1952 as stop-gap motive power until the first of the Beyer articulateds arrived.

One of the 400 class (No. 409) has been preserved at Mile End. Another (No. 402) is with the Zig Zag Tourist Railway at Lithgow, N.S.W.

Principal dimensions

Driving wheels	4 ft 0 in	1219 mm
Cylinders (4)	16 × 24 in	406 × 610 mm
Pressure	200 lb	1379 kPa
Weight	149 tons	151.4 tonnes
Tractive effort	43,250 lb	19 618 kg

Built 1953

AUSTRALIAN NATIONAL RAILWAYS
2. Northern Region
(Ex-Commonwealth Railways)
1914

When the Commonwealth Railways farewelled the last ten-wheeler in 1955 it was the close of an era during which Australia's federally owned rail system could not claim to have devised or built one steam locomotive of its own. Instead, in 40 years of dependency on steam traction on narrow and standard gauges the C.R. achieved its purpose by carefully and conservatively selecting from the ranks of engines developed on other systems. Pioneer passenger locomotive at the opening of the Trans-Australia line in 1917 was the stalwart G class, in effect a direct copy of the N.S.W.R.'s P6 (C32), built by Toowoomba Foundry, Clyde Engineering and Baldwin of U.S.A. A total of 26 Gs were purchased for the Transcontinental between 1914 and 1917, and those of the earlier years, stationed at Port Augusta and Kalgoorlie, took part in actual construction of the historic line.

With running gear scarred by wild dust storms of the Nullarbor Plain and boiler tubes pitted by poor quality water containing scale-forming salts, many of these locomotives were in no shape to contend with the difficult climatic conditions of the then 1691-km (1051-mile) route. Consideration was given to building a new C.R. passenger engine—probably a 4-6-2—but the decision went in favour of economizing, and funds were allocated to repair the battered Gs instead.

On the freight roster, the first eight K class were

Unspectacular but dependable, the K-class copy of N.S.W.'s D53 standard goods.

North British repeats of the N.S.W.R.'s standard goods, while 26 consolidations of the Ka class, supplied by Walkers, Qld, and Perry, S.A., were duplicates of the D53.

For the Port Pirie–Port Augusta extension of 1937 which eliminated South Australia's narrow gauge from the Transcontinental connection, the C.R. looked towards a more powerful passenger engine to maintain

C.R.'s gesture to streamlining—boiler cowling on an oil-fired C class.

an accelerated schedule. Again the selection favoured a proven N.S.W.R. design—the C36 ten-wheeler; eight locos, known as C class, were delivered from Walkers in early 1938. However, C.R. designers did make a dramatic addition to the Transcontinental version of the "Pig"—a 12-wheel tender, which in fact was longer than the loco itself.

The only non-Australian designs to appear on C.R. standard gauge hurriedly arrived to meet the emergency of World War II: eight Cns hailed from the Canadian National Railways and two Cas were ex-New York, New Haven and Hartford Railroad, both 4-6-0s.

As a stop-gap measure before going diesel, the C.R. took delivery of ten surplus Mikados, designated L class, which as copies of the S.A.R. 700s had been commissioned by UNRRA for China's standard gauge: the Communist victory put an end to the Chinese delivery. Unfortunately on the C.R. they eventually arrived too late for useful employment and some were never steamed.

On the 1067-mm (3 ft 6 in) North and Central Australian lines, the C.R. was heir to small six-coupled locos of the South Australian administration, some of which (such as the NF) dated back to 1877. The C.R. contented itself on the light narrow gauge with selecting from the range of Q.R. motive power, most importantly, on the Central Australia route, the NM—a renamed 1924-era C17.

Gauge 1435 mm (4 ft 8½ in)

PASSENGER TYPE

1914   G Class   4-6-0

For the arduous motive-power tasks anticipated on the Trans-Australian line, the Commonwealth Govern-

The Trans-Australian G class, a repeat of N.S.W.'s successful P6.

ment turned to the proven P6 (later C32 class) of New South Wales. These uncomplicated and efficient machines had become the N.S.W.R.'s main passenger work horses since 1892, and as the gauge was identical the choice seemed satisfactory.

A total of 26 locomotives known as G class were built—12 by Baldwin Locomotive Works, 10 by Toowoomba Foundry and 4 by Clyde Engineering—between 1914 and the opening of the line in 1917.

The G continued to handle the main passenger trains under extreme climatic conditions until the arrival of the larger C class 4-6-0s in 1938. The chief modifications made to the class, apart from tests with a feed water heater, were superheaters and enlarged cylinders fitted to the seven which were designated GA.

In 1932–3 the Gs began the longest unbroken loco runs in Australia, from Port Augusta to Cook, 824 km (512 miles) and on to Kalgoorlie, 860 km (539 miles). The same engines were "thrashed" during World War II, and by 1945–6 most were fit for the junk track, although a few continued as shunters until the 1950s.

Class leader G1 is the only standard-gauge locomotive at the Mile End Museum.

Principal dimensions (see also C32 class, N.S.W.R., p. 59)

Driving wheels	5 ft 0 in	1524 mm
Cylinders	20 × 26 in	508 × 660 mm
Pressure	160 lb	1103 kPa
Weight	106 tons	107.7 tonnes
Tractive effort	22,200 lb	10 070 kg

Built 1914–17

1938 C Class 4-6-0

Few locomotives can boast a tender that is longer and heavier than the engine proper.

The Commonwealth Railways used eight of these handsome locomotives with massive tenders on the Trans-Australian line from 1938 until they were displaced by main-line diesels in the early 1950s. The locomotives, known as the C class, were virtu-

From Walkers of Maryborough, Queensland, the 1938 C class was a copy of the N.S.W.R. C36, and had a massive 12-wheel tender.

ally the same (except for the tenders) as the N.S.W.R.'s very successful C36-class passenger express locomotives (see page 64).

The C.R. locos were built by Walkers Ltd and the tenders were required to carry over 54 553 litres (12,000 gallons) of water and 17.3 tonnes (17 tons) of coal for the long hops between major watering and fuelling points across the Nullarbor Plain, principally Port Augusta–Cook and Cook–Kalgoorlie, a total stretch of almost 1700 km.

The tenders were so big that they had to be constructed in the shipyard which adjoined Walker's loco-assembling plant at their Maryborough (Qld) works. During the coal crisis, five Cs were converted to oil fuel, the tenders being fitted with a 15 911-litre (3500-gallon) bunker.

After the C-class scrapping, some of the tenders were retained and used on weed-poisoning trains on the Trans-Australian Railway.

Principal dimensions (see also C36 class, N.S.W.R., p. 64)

Driving wheels	5 ft 9 in	1753 mm
Cylinders	23 × 26 in	584 × 660 mm
Pressure	180 lb	1241 kPa
Weight	159 tons	161.5 tonnes
Tractive effort	30,500 lb	13 835 kg

Built 1938

1942   Ca/Cn Class   4-6-0

Thankful for any motive power that could turn a wheel during World War II, the Commonwealth Railways briefly operated 10 well-used locos which had seen service in North America. These were purchased in 1942 to augment the Trans-Australian line, which was clogged with wartime traffic. Eight came from the Canadian National Railways, where they had

Wartime imports, the Canadian Cn (top) and American Ca-class ten-wheelers.

given good service for over 30 years, while the other two were from the New York, New Haven and Hartford Railroad, U.S.A.

The Cas were interesting in that they had 1854-mm (6 ft 1 in) driving wheels, one (No. 78) with Southern valve gear and the other (No. 79) with Baker gear. Otherwise they were generally similar in appearance—typical American ten-wheelers—and of about the same tractive power.

The 10 locos were reported to have "seen better days" when they arrived in Australia, although the Canadians were in somewhat sounder condition than their U.S. counterparts. All were immediately pressed into passenger and mixed traffic on the line, but the U.S. locomotives, which had been built by the Baldwin Locomotive Works, lasted only a short time. They were withdrawn in 1945 and 1950. The Canadian locos (built by the Montreal Locomotive Co.) were used until 1951–2.

The C.R. classified these locos as Cn class for the Canadians and Ca class for the two Baldwin products. No member of either class was preserved.

Principal dimensions

Driving wheels	Cn 5 ft 3 in	1600 mm
	Ca 6 ft 1 in	1854 mm
Cylinders	Cn 20½ × 26 in	521 × 660 mm
	Ca 22 × 26 in	559 × 660 mm
Pressure	Cn 200 lb	1379 kPa
	Ca 190 lb	1310 kPa
Weight	Cn 127 tons	129 tonnes
	Ca 131 tons	133 tonnes
Tractive effort	Cn 29,125 lb	13 211 kg
	Ca 27,840 lb	12 628 kg

Built 1905–08

Narrow gauge 1067 mm (3 ft 6 in)

1886   NA Class   0-4-0T

Travellers on the Trans-Australian or Indian-Pacific expresses will have noticed displayed on the platform at Port Augusta a midget locomotive known as "Sandfly". The history of this 1886 Baldwin engine began at the port of Darwin, where it was landed to

"Sandfly"

work on the construction of the North Australia Railway.

"Sandfly" was acquired by the South Australian Railways at the completion of the line and used for jetty and yard shunting. Transferred to Commonwealth ownership in 1911, it continued a humdrum existence in North Australia for almost 60 years until retired in 1970. It was then displayed outside the operating headquarters of the Commonwealth Railways (as the organization was then known).

Principal dimensions

Driving wheels	2 ft 4 in	711 mm
Cylinders	8 × 12 in	203 × 305 mm
Pressure	140 lb	965 kPa
Weight	9 tons	9.1 tonnes
Tractive effort	3,270 lb	1483 kg

Built 1886

1906 NJAB Class 0-4-0T

South Australia's two quaint steam coaches were, in effect, forerunners of the petrol or diesel-powered railcars. They consisted of a tiny steam locomotive complete with boiler, cab and cylinders and an attached 22-seat passenger coach. Commonly referred to as "Coffee-pots", one of them was used on the Mount Gambier–Beachport line and the other between Quorn and Hawker. Kitson & Co. built the locomotive sections, while the bodies came from an English carriage manufacturer.

The unit at Quorn was transferred to Commonwealth Railways ownership when the Federal Government took over the Central Australia line, and it continued to operate variously between Quorn, Hawker and Port Augusta until withdrawn about 1930 and stored at Quorn. Handed to the National Trust, it was displayed at Alice Springs from 1960 to 1975, when the Pichi Richi Railway Preservation group at Quorn assumed responsibility for its restoration to working order.

Kitson 0-4-0 WT, combined loco-carriage; it became NJAB 1 on the C.R.'s narrow gauge.

Principal dimensions

Driving wheels	2 ft 3 in	686 mm
Cylinders	6½ × 10 in	165 × 254 mm
Pressure	170 lb	1172 kPa
Weight	22 tons	22.4 tonnes
Tractive effort	2128 lb	965 kg

Built 1906

1925   NM Class   4-8-0

When it assumed responsibility for the Central Australia line, the Commonwealth Railways adopted a Queensland C17 class as its major engine power. The tough 4-8-0s had performed well on the home tracks and the C.R. order went to Thompson & Co. of Castlemaine, Vic. for 22 engines with very few alterations.

The NMs hauled all kinds of trains between Port Augusta and Alice Springs, including the legendary

NM 22 at Port Augusta with the weekly mixed from Marree.

"Ghan". They were also employed on heavy coal traffic from Leigh Creek to Port Augusta before standard gauge. One (No. 38) was delivered new to Darwin, but was little used owing to the light nature of the North Australia tracks. NM No. 34 has been preserved at Mile End.

Principal dimensions

Driving wheels	3 ft 9 in	1143 mm
Cylinders	17 × 22 in	432 × 559 mm
Pressure	160 lb	1103 kPa
Weight	81 tons	82.3 tonnes
Tractive effort	19,250 lb	8732 kg

Built 1925–27

AUSTRALIAN NATIONAL RAILWAYS
3. Tasmanian Region
(Ex-Tasmanian Government Railways)
1871

Through a chequered railway history, Tasmania has been a locomotive buyer rather than a builder. The complex pattern of railway development in the small island State resulted in a fascinating variety of motive power in which some of the more complex types of yesteryear made their appearance on 1067-mm (3 ft 6 in) and 610-mm (2-ft) metals that at one time were part of the T.G.R. empire. Though broad gauge had been selected for the first railway opened in 1874 between Launceston and Deloraine, a switch to the more practical narrow dimension was made by the mid-1880s. (After all, what does break-of-gauge matter to a Tasmanian?)

While the government went ahead with its own independent system, the private Tasmanian Main Line Co. in 1874 completed the 214 km (133 miles) Hobart–Launceston route (with third-rail running rights north of Deloraine); farther afield, the resourceful Emu Bay and Mt Lyell companies made the mountainous west coast almost wholly a private railway preserve—except for the short stretch of government track that joined them both. From the T.M.L. at the takeover of 1890, the government system acquired a fleet of four- and six-coupled Dubs and Hunslet engines; from the original private broad gauge in 1891 it converted a Sharp Stewart passenger engine to a unique narrow-gauge 4-2-2. In its loco

Tasmanian steam railways began in 1871 with the broad-gauge Launceston & Western.

acquisitions the T.G.R. shopped from builders both well and lesser known—in Australia particularly from Walkers of Maryborough, Qld, and Perry of S.A., and from other operators secondhand.

For the enthusiast much of the appeal of this small railway system lay in the fact that many of these engines—dare one call them a motley collection?—could not be found elsewhere; they were special to Tasmania. In any such listing, pride of place immediately goes to the two tiny K class, the world's first Beyer Garratts (and 0-4-0 + 0-4-0 compounds as well, with cylinders at the bogie inboard ends), which were bravely purchased for the 610-mm (2-ft) North-East Dundas Tramway in 1909. Three years later the T.G.R. went to the other extreme in articulation and ordered the world's first double-Atlantic express Garratts, high stepping engines capable of 97 km/h (60 mph) on the Hobart–Launceston express, and driven by eight cylinders—two outside and two inside at each end. A more mundane buy of the same period was a six-coupled L-class Garratt to pull goods trains. For suburban running the T.G.R.

imported eight DS-class 2-6-4Ts secondhand from the New Zealand Railways in 1939; these were the only N.Z.-built engines to be used on an Australian government line.

Beyer, Peacock held almost a monopoly on new engines in the early 1900s and, apart from the Garratts, delivered the predictable 4-4-0 and 2-6-0, some of which went through the usual rebuilds. No pant of air pump resounded from any of these locos for, like Western Australia, the T.G.R. remained with the English vacuum brake. Alone of all Australian railways, the system also kept the Americans at bay and (except for a couple of ex-contractor or constructions engines) neither the Baldwin nor any other U.S. builder's plate was ever seen in a Tasmanian shed.

Gauge 1067 mm (3 ft 6 in)

PASSENGER TYPE

1892　　A Class　　4-4-0

The earliest rail services in Tasmania were provided by private companies, although the Government was forced to acquire these small organizations when financial problems threatened to overwhelm them.

Beyer, Peacock built eight of the comely 4-4-0s for the Tasmanian Government Railways to meet engine-power needs on the main line to Launceston and the Western line to Deloraine (and beyond) after these routes passed into the department's control. The As handled passenger services until they were displaced by the more spectacular M-class Beyer Garratts in 1912.

Gradually the class was improved with Belpaire boilers and larger fireboxes, although they were transferred to branch and shunting duties. All were

Beyer, Peacock 4-4-0 A class, Tasmania's main-line passenger horse of the 1900s.

withdrawn in 1950; one (No. 4) was retained and today can be found on display in a Launceston park.

Principal dimensions

Driving wheels	4 ft 7 in	1397 mm
Cylinders	$15\frac{1}{2} \times 22$ in	394×559 mm
Pressure	150 lb	1034 kPa
Weight	53 tons	53.8 tonnes
Tractive effort	11,530 lb	5230 kg

Built 1892–1902

1912   M Class   4-4-2 + 2-4-4

Only three years after the world's first Beyer Garratts were built for the T.G.R., the system again made history by ordering the first Garratts in the world for fast passenger working. These were the M-class "double Atlantics" with a total of eight cylinders—four inside and four outside.

T.G.R.'s "double Atlantic" M class, first Garratt built for express passenger traffic.

One M class achieved fame when it broke the early world speed record for an articulated locomotive with a burst of 85 km/h (53 mph)—a speed which would have been respectable even for a conventional loco on narrow-gauge tracks.

The M class principally worked the Main line between Launceston and Hobart. They were withdrawn about 1930 and eventually cut up for scrap.

Principal dimensions
Driving wheels	5 ft 0 in	1524 mm
Cylinders (8)	12 × 20 in	305 × 508 mm
Pressure	160 lb	1103 kPa
Weight	95 tons	96.5 tonnes
Tractive effort	24,576 lb	11 147 kg

Built 1912

1923   R Class   4-6-2

Perry Engineering Co. of South Australia built four Pacifics in 1922 to replace the elderly 4-4-0 power then in use. Classified R, they were used for passenger services on the Main line, as well as the Western, Derwent Valley and Fingal branches; express trains were managed on 1-in-40 grade without loss of time. For several years one loco (R4) was fitted with a

R-class No. 4 once carried streamlining for Hobart–Launceston expresses.

streamlined casing similar to the Victorian Railways' S class, in an effort to increase public patronage during the depression years of the 1930s.

No example of the T.G.R.'s first Pacifics is preserved. All were withdrawn and scrapped by 1959.

Principal dimensions

Driving wheels	4 ft 7 in	1397 mm
Cylinders	20 × 24 in	508 × 610 mm
Pressure	160 lb	1103 kPa
Weight	98 tons	99.6 tonnes
Tractive effort	23,790 lb	10 791 kg

Built 1923

1952 M Class 4-6-2

The second M class were also Tasmania's second Pacifics acquired after World War II. The 10 locos were delivered in 1952 from Robert Stephenson & Hawthorns Ltd, and closely followed a design used on the Indian Railways. Though they had been intended for passenger trains, the entry of the M class locos coincided with the arrival of the new diesel power and they were rarely given top link assignments. Four were later fitted with smaller wheels retrieved from the ASGs, to allow them to handle heavier goods trains on the steep grades of the North-East line; these engines were reclassified Ma. All 10 were withdrawn during the 1960s (although two were retained for steam-cleaning purposes).

One (M3) has been upgraded for enthusiast trains and another (M6) is now at the Bellarine Railway, Queenscliff. Those on display in Tasmania are at Granton (Ma1), Ross (M1) and Stanley (M2). The Van Diemen Light Railway Society in Don has acquired Ma2.

Principal dimensions

Driving wheels	4 ft 7 in	1397 mm
	Ma 4 ft 0 in	1219 mm
Cylinders	16 × 24 in	406 × 610 mm
Pressure	180 lb	1241 kPa
Weight	96½ tons	98 tonnes
	Ma 95 tons	96.5 tonnes
Tractive effort	17,090 lb	7752 kg
	Ma 19,584 lb	8883 kg

Built 1952

GOODS TYPE

1885   C Class   2-6-0

Most Australian narrow-gauge systems acquired locomotives of the same Beyer, Peacock design that the T.G.R. selected in the 1880s for the recently re-

Vintage train loco CCS 23 double-heading with Ma-class Pacific on a T.G.R. centenary special.

gauged Deloraine line. Tasmania's 2-6-0s, classified C, were delivered between 1885 and 1892. The 19 in the class soon achieved a reputation for reliability and hard work on goods trains, their light axle load making them suited to all lines. Eight more Cs were purchased from Beyer, Peacock several years later. In 1912 the T.G.R. commenced a loco improvement programme and six Cs, fitted with Belpaire boilers and larger smokeboxes, were reclassified CC.

Further conversions were made in the 1920s when four more C class were equipped with Belpaire boilers and Walschaert valve gear; these were known as the CCS class.

The Emu Bay Railway Co. acquired three C class from the same builder, while another was transferred to the T.G.R. roster in the 1930s after it had been used on construction work for many years.

One CCS class (23) has been retained for enthusiast trains; C22 is preserved at the Transport Museum, Hobart, and C1 is in Zeehan.

Principal dimensions
Driving wheels   3 ft 3 in   991 mm

Cylinders	14½ × 20 in	368 × 508 mm
CCS	15 × 20 in	381 × 508 mm
Pressure	145 lb	1000 kPa
CCS	175 lb	1207 kPa
Weight	47½ tons	48.3 tonnes
CCS	56 tons	56.9 tonnes
Tractive effort	12,507 lb	5673 kg
CCS	13,660 lb	6196 kg

Built 1885–1902

1912   L Class   2-6-2 + 2-6-2

The T.G.R.'s early enthusiasm for Garratts included the purchase of two articulated locomotives for freight duty in 1912, at the same time as the M-class double Atlantics arrived. The 2-6-2 + 2-6-2 L class were considerably more powerful than any engines then in use. They worked the Main line from Hobart to Launceston and occasionally took over the passenger turns despite the small wheels.

The L-class Garratt, a close copy of the M, but with smaller driving wheels and four cylinders.

The Ls were withdrawn in 1930 but not scrapped; they returned to service briefly during World War II. Regrettably, neither was kept for preservation.

Principal dimensions

Driving wheels	3 ft 6 in	1067 mm
Cylinders (4)	15 × 22 in	381 × 559 mm
Pressure	160 lb	1103 kPa
Weight	90 tons	91.4 tonnes
Tractive effort	30,170 lb	13 685 kg

Built 1912

1922 Q Class 4-8-2

In the early 1920s the T.G.R. turned to a 4-8-2 Mountain type as its main freight power. The first six were supplied by Perry Engineering Co. of South Australia in 1922 and classified Q. Three more came from Walkers Ltd in 1929. Clyde Engineering Co. built 10 between 1936 and 1945. Generally the locos were limited to the heaviest tracks, including the Main line and the Fingal and Derwent Valley branches.

The last four, Q16–Q19, were fitted with boilers

Three Australian makers contributed to the principal freight loco, the Mountain Q class.

having a pressure raised from 1103 kPa (160 lb) to 1241 kPa (180 lb), which increased tractive effort by 1542 kg (3400 lb).

The last Q ceased operation in 1964. One has been preserved in Hobart—actually Q5, although it has been numbered Q1 for historical significance.

Principal dimensions
Driving wheels	4 ft 0 in	1219 mm
Cylinders	20 × 24 in	508 × 610 mm
Pressure	160 lb	1103 kPa
Weight	98 tons	99.6 tonnes
Tractive effort	27,200 lb	12 338 kg

Built 1922–45

1951   H Class   4-8-2

When time could not be spared to evolve a new design, the T.G.R. agreed to buy a locomotive type which had been supplied earlier to the African Gold Coast.

Vulcan Foundry delivered the eight H class in 1951. Once again it was an instance of capable steam locos arriving at about the same time as rival diesel power. However, the H was used to advantage on the Main, Fingal and Western lines and later in the north-west.

Two were out of service by 1962 and the rest joined them prematurely on the scrap track. Two were refurbished for the T.G.R.'s centenary celebrations in 1971 and one (No. 2) was retained for enthusiast excursions.

Principal dimensions
Driving wheels	4 ft 0 in	1219 mm
Cylinders	18 × 24 in	457 × 610 mm
Pressure	200 lb	1379 kPa
Weight	111 tons	112.8 tonnes

Last of the T.G.R.'s big power, the 4-8-2 H class.

Tractive effort   27,540 lb   12 492 kg

Built 1951

Narrow gauge 610 mm (2 ft)

1909   K Class   0-4-0 + 0-4-0

The Tasmanian Government Railways were the first in the world to purchase a Beyer Garratt locomotive. Admittedly the two K class delivered from Manchester in 1909 were of midget proportions: however, their home was to be in the remote West Coast on the system's 610-mm (2-ft) gauge North-East Dundas Tramway. The K class were unique in having the cylinders inboard on the bogie sets. (All later Beyer

The original Garratt—Tasmania's K1.

Garratts were built with cylinders at the outer ends.) They were also compound locomotives; the two cylinders at the smokebox end were high pressure while the low pressure cylinders, of different diameter, were at the cab end.

Fluctuating business in the mining industry forced the retirement of the Ks in 1938 and they were placed in store. Beyer, Peacock acquired class leader K1 in 1947 and placed it on display at the company's Gorton Foundry; parts from K2 were used in the reconstruction of K1.

When the Beyer, Peacock plant closed in the late 1960s, K1 was sold to the 597-mm (1 ft 11½ in) gauge Festiniog tourist railway in Wales, and it is now on loan to the National Railway Museum, York.

Principal dimensions

Driving wheels	2 ft 7½ in	800 mm
Cylinders (high)	11 × 16 in	279 × 406 mm
(low)	17 × 16 in	432 × 406 mm
Pressure	195 lb	1345 kPa
Weight	33½ tons	34 tonnes
Tractive effort	18,000 lb	8165 kg

Built 1909

QUEENSLAND RAILWAYS
1865

Six years after the proclamation of Queensland as a separate colony, the first train ran to Bigge's Camp (Grandchester) at the foot of the Little Liverpool Range, a distance of 33 km (20½ miles). By intention the Queensland Railways was government property from that inauguration day of 31 July 1865. Another matter of difference from the older southern lines was the starting point, which was not the capital Brisbane, but the river town of Ipswich, some 40 km (25 miles) upstream. In Queensland the name of Ipswich was to become firmly linked with the steam locomotive for practically a century—"Ipswich designed" ... "built at Ipswich Railway Workshops" ... "modified at Ipswich Shops" ... and so on.

How does one briefly encompass the locomotive developments of the far-flung Queensland network, on which—to give an idea of the distances involved—it is possible within State borders to make a regular passenger train journey of 2300 km (1429 miles) from Brisbane to Mount Isa? From the mid-1860s the railway established itself in some seven isolated sections, most of which struck inland from a coastal terminus; for a considerable time the slender resources of these separate lines dictated that engine power should be small and simple to repair and even in later years Q.R. locos retained a "divisional" identity far more pronounced than that of other systems.

Early locomotives came from Britain. "Faugh-a-Ballagh" was the first 2-4-0 from Avonside to sound its whistle on Ipswich wharf. The pioneer A10s were

The old Q.R. steam depot at Mayne Junction, Brisbane.

joined by 0-4-2s from Neilson. If locos were decidedly dinky, motive-power policy was also reasonably adventurous: in 1871 a lone 8D11 double-four coupled Fairlie was imported to struggle up the Range. By 1878–9, graceful Baldwin eight-wheelers and chunky Consolidations that may well have been copied from the Denver and Rio Grande were working on the system. Right up to the demise of steam, the Q.R. built many of its own engines in the government workshops and bought others from a wide variety of makers at home and overseas. In the 100 years to 1965, of the total of 1311 steam locos put into service, no less than 908 originated within the State. Many of them carried builders' plates little seen elsewhere, such as the Phoenix Engine Co., Ipswich, and Evans, Anderson & Phelan & Co.—who sent their engines down the street from South Brisbane dragged by horses on portable sections of track. Among more widely known makers were Walkers of Maryborough, who in the 61 years to 1958 completed 449 locos.

The first Engineer-in-Chief and Commissioner, Irishman Abram Fitzgibbon, once said of the Q.R.: "It is far better to go 500 miles at 15 mph than 250

At Warwick in 1891, A12 4-4-0 No. 258 heads the main-line passenger train.

miles at 25 mph." Here in a nutshell was government policy—to bring transport as quickly as possible to the great outback spaces and the long coastal stretches, and to achieve it on a limited budget by employing lots of low-powered utility locomotives that would skim over lightweight rail, negotiate spindly-legged trestle bridges and surmount the sharpest curves and grades. Light axle loads and low driving wheels were the hallmark of Q.R. engines. Gradually the original 8.1-tonne (8-ton) axle limit of H. Horniblow's "go-anywhere" PB15s was raised to 9.1 tonnes (9 tons) to allow for the design of another C.M.E., G. Nutt, whose C16 twelve-wheeler of 1901 developed 25 per cent greater tractive effort.

The demands of Brisbane suburban lines, oddly divided between the northside and the south, made Q.R. a leader in tank loco development, of which C.M.E. W. H. Nisbet's 6D16 was another 1901 milestone—a 4-6-2T (later 4-6-4T) imposing for the first time a 12.2-tonne (12-ton) axle weight. (Q.R. locos were classified by "A" for 4-coupled, "B" for 6-coupled and "D" for tanks, with the following number indicating cylinder diameter. In the case of

PB15 in the steam days of the famous Grandstand train from Cairns.

tanks, the driving-wheel figure was also sometimes placed ahead of the "D", another Queensland peculiarity.) Driving-wheel size went from 914 mm (36 in) on early B15s to 1143 mm (45 in) on the C16s and C17s, then to 1295 mm (51 in) on the later main-line locos—and there it stayed. This amalgam of ancestry and track limitations produced the essential "Q.R." engine, with its long-framed cowcatcher, brassbound boiler, tall stack with raised front lip, Johnson bar reverse lever, pull-out regulator and cutaway cab—whose design did not alter for some 45 years—and, of course, the inseparable organ-reed "peanut" whistle.

Loco speeds were rarely urged above 80 km/h (50 mph) and tractive effort in 85 years of steam running, despite the introduction of the heavy goods C18s and C19s of the 1914–22 era to battle the 1-in-45 grades of the Main Range, did not rise above 10 886 kg (24,000 lb). Not until 1950, in fact, did the Beyer Garratts appear (and Beyer, Peacock was one company that had made little penetration into the Q.R. market), having an output more comparable to that of the larger locos used on other narrow gauges. But versatility was the name of the game in Queensland. The B18¼ Pacific was produced in 1926 to run main-line trains, including the Sunshine Express of the recently linked-up 1679-km (1043 miles) North Coast route. But stand on Central Station in the 1950s, when steam was still king, and watch for the next suburban to Sandgate. It might be a trim blue DD17 tank; on the other hand, it could be a BB18¼ with roller bearings—not on the express today, thanks, but all shining and green.

Gauge 1067 mm (3 ft 6 in)

PASSENGER TYPE

1865   A10 Class   0-4-2

The second class of locomotives on the Queensland Railways were the four small 0-4-2s imported from Neilson & Co. of Glasgow in 1865. They were the motive power for the opening section of the Queensland system, which commenced that year between Ipswich and Grandchester. As traffic improved, a further 12 were ordered the next year. With their four-wheel tenders, these "Tiny Tims" were soon outclassed by larger engines and vacated the main line for other duties. Some were sold and most remaining with the Q.R. were written off by 1900.

The survivor at the Redbank Museum (No. 6) had an interesting career, being sold to the Bingera Sugar Mill in 1895 where it was used for seasonal cane traffic until 1965—its 101st year. For the Q.R.'s centenary celebrations, Bingera management handed it over to the Commissioner for future preservation. Another class member (No. 3) was stored at Ipswich from 1914, but steamed again at the celebrations of 1936. This loco then went on display for over 20

No. 6 is one of two A10-class 0-4-2s to survive for over a century.

years at Roma Street, Brisbane's main long-distance station, and it is now preserved in a park at Ipswich.

Principal dimensions

Driving wheels	3 ft 0 in	914 mm
Cylinders	10 × 18 in	254 × 457 mm
Pressure	120 lb	827 kPa
Weight	22½ tons	22.9 tonnes
Tractive effort	4,800 lb	2177 kg

Built 1865–6

1882 A12/A14 Class 4-4-0

Queensland's first U.S.-built locomotives were acquired in 1878. The A12s were typical American-style 4-4-0s which, with their leading truck, were expected to perform well in passenger service on the light narrow gauge.

Baldwin Works supplied three of the locos, at

the same time as a batch of Consolidations for goods service. In 1882 they delivered a further 18 improved A12s.

The old Yankees were quite impressive engines for their day and carried the usual adornment of diamond stacks and canister-type sand and steam domes, plus a "flivver" four-wheel tender which appeared almost as an afterthought. Between 1890 and 1891 the Brisbane firm of Evans, Anderson & Phelan supplied a further 25 to the U.S. pattern, while at Ipswich the Phoenix works in 1894 built eight locos of the larger A14 dimension.

The Q.R. had its share of "Yankee" influence: the A14 was a local development of the Baldwin 4-4-0.

All As gave good service on passenger, freight and mixed services on the isolated sections of the system, but they were eventually displaced by six-coupled locomotives. One lasted until 1929, but none has been preserved.

Principal dimensions

Driving wheels	4 ft 0 in	1219 mm
Cylinders	12 × 18 in	305 × 457 mm
Pressure	120 lb	827 kPa
Weight	33 tons	33.5 tonnes
Tractive effort	4,860 lb	2204 kg

Built 1882–91

1883 B13 Class 4-6-0

Though a lightly powered workhorse, the B13 represented Queensland's first serious move towards the ten-wheel type loco, and as such was the forerunner of a long line of small engines with which the Q.R. became identified.

In all, 112 were built, starting in 1883 with the first 19 from Dubs & Co., Glasgow, which were sent to the then numerous isolated sections of the system.

Further orders were placed with Dubs & Co. (52), Kitson & Co. (26), and the Phoenix Foundry at Ipswich (15). The early models had open cabs and some were equipped initially with balloon stacks to burn wood.

Various modifications were made during the life of the B13 as it continued to prove useful on branch lines for freight and mixed duties. Six were sold to the Commonwealth Railways in 1913 where they were classified NG.

Withdrawals started in 1919, although a number of B13s sold to sugar mills lasted much longer than those remaining on the government system. One also operated the scenic Beaudesert Tramway, and after retirement was cut up at Woolloongabba loco yards.

B13 class on the now defunct Beaudesert Tramway, followed by a unique Foden loco.

No. 48, which has been preserved at Redbank, was a sugar-mill engine donated back to the Q.R. in 1967.

Principal dimensions

Driving wheels	3 ft 3 in	991 mm
Cylinders	13 × 20 in	330 × 508 mm
Pressure	150 lb	1034 kPa
Weight	50 tons	50.8 tonnes
Tractive effort	10,400 lb	4717 kg

Built 1883–92

1889/1903   B15 Con Class   4-6-0

In 1889 the Q.R. introduced the first of its large and heavier fleet of 4-6-0 locomotives for freight operations. Regarded as big power for the times, these B15s were supplied by Nasmyth Wilson & Co. (15), Evans, Anderson & Phelan (21), Yorkshire Engine Co. (10) and Walkers Ltd (46). Searching for improved passenger motive power, the department initiated in 1903 a conversion on all but five of the 98 locos to a "B15 Con" class fitted with larger driving wheels and increased boiler pressure.

The original Walkers B15 4-6-0 goods loco.

Six B15 class which were built for the Chillagoe Railway & Mining Co. ultimately passed to Q.R. ownership. The B15 "converteds" spent most of their working life on passenger, freight and mixed trains in the northern part of the State until overtaken by the larger engines.

No. 290 finished its days as a shunter at Rockhampton and in 1968 was withdrawn for preservation at the Redbank Rail Museum. A B15 Con Class (299) is preserved at Walkers, Maryborough.

Principal dimensions

Driving wheels	3 ft 9 in	1143 mm
Cylinders	15 × 20 in	381 × 508 mm
Pressure	160 lb	1103 kPa
Weight	55 tons	55.9 tonnes
Tractive effort	14,770 lb	6700 kg

Built 1903

1899 PB15 Class   4-6-0

The PB15, intended for passenger and mixed traffic, became a most widely used locomotive.

The first was completed by Walkers Ltd in 1899; 202 had been built by 1912. The PBs were intended for mail and passenger operations, but as the years wore on they took to all types of haulage including suburban, freight and shunting. Virtually every branch on the Q.R. system at some time or other operated a PB15.

The design was modified in the 1920s and a further 30 were built in 1925–6 with Walschaert valve gear instead of Stephenson inside motion.

An engine constructed for the Aramac Tramway in 1925 also came into the Q.R.'s ranks. As small ten-wheelers the PBs were capable of quite extraordinary haulage feats. They also made some legendary fast

Typical PB 15, brass-banded 444 as the class first appeared in 1899.

runs, such as those with the old South Brisbane-to-Southport seaside expresses.

After final scrapping in the late 1960s, four have been retained: two (Nos 732 and 738) for enthusiast trains and No. 444 at Redbank, while No. 454 has travelled far afield and is preserved by the Geelong Steam Preservation Society for the Bellarine Peninsula line.

No. 737, one of the Walschaert PBs that ran "Davidson's Baby" and other long-departed South Coast trains.

Principal dimensions

Driving wheels	4 ft 0 in	1219 mm
Cylinders	15 × 20 in	381 × 508 mm
Pressure	160 lb	1103 kPa
Weight	56 tons	56.9 tonnes
Tractive effort	12,000 lb	5443 kg

Built 1899–1926

1926   B18¼ Class   4-6-2

The impending link-up of the final isolated parts of the 1600-km (1000-mile) North Coast line in 1924 prompted the Q.R. to took towards a more capable and specialized passenger locomotive. For the first time the department also adopted the Pacific wheel arrangement

Sunshine Express power, the B18¼, Q.R.'s first main-line Pacific.

in the 17 locos that appeared from Ipswich Workshops between 1926 and 1930 and the further six of a slightly modified design that followed in 1935.

In 1936 the Q.R. took delivery of what was to be regarded as the first of 60 "standard" B18¼s, with larger tenders, an improved "sedan" cab and more efficient boilers. The last of this standard version, which was built by Ipswich Shops and Walkers Ltd, was not delivered until 1947.

The B18¼s ran top link passenger and mail trains, as well as the important fruit expresses. In later years they took over mixed duties on freights, shunting and even ballast trains. The class was gradually written off during the 1950s and 1960s.

In operating condition, No. 843 has been retained by the Q.R. for fan and excursion trains, and another (No. 771) is on display at the Redbank Museum.

Principal dimensions

Driving wheels	4 ft 3 in	1295 mm
Cylinders	18¼ × 26 in	464 × 660 mm
Pressure	170 lb	1172 kPa
Weight	93 tons	94.5 tonnes
Tractive effort	22,650 lb	10 274 kg

Built 1926–47

1951   BB18¼ Class   4-6-2

Based on the successful B18¼, a subsequent class of 55 more modern passenger locomotives was introduced in 1951. The improvements on the earlier design included roller-bearing axleboxes and siderods, cleaner steam passages and larger tenders. The first 35 were imported from the Vulcan Foundry of U.K., to be followed in 1955 with the first of 20 built locally by Walkers Ltd. The latter order, completed in 1958, represented the last steam locomotives for an Aus-

BB18¼ class, the 1951 development of the original Pacifics.

tralian government railway.

Popular with engine crews, the responsive BB18¼s handled major passenger trains, particularly from Brisbane, Toowoomba and Rockhampton, and also did their turn on the northside suburban trains.

In common with the companion B18¼s, the Pacifics appeared in the Q.R.'s postwar livery of attractive hawthorn green.

Two have been retained by the Queensland Railways for fan and special trips—Nos 1079 and 1072. The last BB18¼-class locomotive (No. 1089) is displayed at the Redbank Museum. Other preservations are at Winton (No. 1077) and Mackay (No. 1037).

Principal dimensions

Driving wheels	4 ft 3 in	1295 mm
Cylinders	18¼ × 24 in	464 × 610 mm
Pressure	170 lb	1172 kPa
Weight	101 tons	102.6 tonnes
Tractive effort	22,650 lb	10 274 kg

Built 1951–8

GOODS TYPE

1903 C16 Class 4-8-0

Though Baldwin consolidations of the C16 grouping had been used since 1882, the engines which followed C.M.E. Nutt's 1901 design marked the Q.R.'s entry into providing a freight loco best suited to the demands of the light axle-load system.

Now at Redbank Museum, No. 106 of class C16.

After introduction in 1903, the 157 class members were built, up to 1918, by Ipswich Workshops (51), Walkers Ltd (45), Toowoomba Foundry (15), and Evans, Anderson & Phelan (41). Apart from goods and livestock trains, the C16s were also assigned to some of the top passenger runs on the Main Range grades, including the Mails.

Modifications were effected during the 1930s and 11 were lent to the Commonwealth during World War II; they were listed as NMBs on the Central Australia Railway.

Though scrapping began in 1934, most of the class were running in the late 1960s when dieselization soon reduced their numbers; the last was withdrawn in 1970. No. 106 has been preserved at Redbank.

Principal dimensions

Driving wheels	3 ft 9 in	1143 mm
Cylinders	16 × 22 in	406 × 559 mm
Pressure	170 lb	1172 kPa
Weight	80 tons	81.3 tonnes
Tractive effort	18,085 lb	8203 kg

Built 1903–18

1920   C17 Class   4-8-0

Designed by the Q.R.'s engineering team, Messrs Robertson and Pemberton, the C17 was launched in 1920 as a superheated version of the C16. It was to become the system's most successful freight motive power and its most prolific class.

The twelve-wheelers were delivered in batches for the next 33 years, the last (No. 1000) being completed by Walkers in 1953, when the class totalled 226. The design was adopted by the Commonwealth Railways for 22 NM-class locomotives on the Central Australia line.

The C17 class proved highly versatile: while performing extremely well in their intended sphere of goods and mixed operations, they were also to be seen on passenger, mail and suburban trains.

When the first C17s were being built, the Q.R.'s habit was to re-allocate road numbers from discarded motive power, which explains why the two members of the class which have been preserved at Redbank Museum carry such widely varying plates as "2" and "1000". A splendid brown livery was adopted in postwar times.

The class gradually succumbed to diesels in the 1950s, and by 1970 only one (No. 974) had been retained for fan operations.

Other C17s on display throughout the State are at

C17 twelve-wheeler No. 861 on a Pinkenba suburban.

Gympie (Nos 45 and 820), Atherton (812), Blackwater (980), Caloundra (967), Cairns (988), Charters Towers (251), Chinchilla (97), Cloncurry (779), Gladstone (965), Goondiwindi (720), Injune (824), Jandowae (719), Mundubbera (253), Miles (944), Mitchell (761), Paddington (763), Brisbane (705), Roma (802), Southport (996), Virginia (935), Yeppoon (966).

Principal dimensions

Driving wheels	3 ft 9 in	1143 mm
Cylinders	17 × 22 in	432 × 559 mm
Pressure	175 lb	1207 kPa
Weight	83 tons	84.3 tonnes
Tractive effort	21,000 lb	9525 kg

Built 1920–53

1922 C19 Class 4-8-0

When introduced in 1922, the Queensland Railways' C19 was claimed to be the world's biggest engine for 1067-mm (3 ft 6 in) gauge. The long-firebox design was intended to surmount the 1-in-45 grades of the Main Range and to negotiate the slopes of other

Q.R.'s largest conventional steam power, the superheated C19.

sections of the Southern, Northern and Western lines where difficult terrain was encountered.

Though basically a freight engine, the C19 was equally successful on major passenger and mail trains. The design developed from a superheated version of the C18-class 4-8-0s—the "Macgregors" of 1914—which were originally introduced to haul the "Sydney Mail" in the days of the Wallangarra break-of-gauge interstate route.

Twenty C19s were built by Ipswich Workshops from 1922 and a further six from Walkers Ltd up to 1935. The three C18 locos were superheated and converted in 1934 to a "CC19", making 29 big freight engines in all.

The last C19 was withdrawn in 1964, but one class member (700) has been preserved at Redbank.

Principal dimensions

Driving wheels	4 ft 0 in	1219 mm
Cylinders	19 × 23 in	483 × 584 mm
Pressure	160 lb	1103 kPa
Weight	97 tons	98.6 tonnes
Tractive effort	23,525 lb	10 671 kg

Built 1922–35

1943   AC16 Class   2-8-2

The AC16 was a lend-lease engine provided from U.S. Army stocks to assist the beleaguered Q.R. system in the motive-power crisis of World War II. The Baldwin Locomotive Works, U.S.A. supplied the 20 Mikados, similar to hundreds of other engines provided for such countries as Greece, India and Thailand. Eventually the Q.R. made an outright purchase of their latest "Yankees".

Baldwin flavour returned to Q.R. with the AC16 Mikado of World War II.

Rugged in appearance, the AC16s were used chiefly on freights, although they were sometimes tried on passenger trains. At higher speeds problems were experienced with the riding of the tenders and a speed limit was imposed until 1959, when they were equipped with spare C16 tenders. The AC16s were then cleared for passenger working and took their turn at times on the Midlander and other named air-conditioned expresses. All were laid aside by 1969. No. 221A has been preserved at the Redbank Rail Museum with its original American-built tender; No. 218A has been acquired by the Zig Zag Railway Co-operative, N.S.W.

Principal dimensions

Driving wheels	4 ft 0 in	1219 mm
Cylinders	16 × 24 in	406 × 610 mm
Pressure	185 lb	1276 kPa
Weight	94 tons	95.5 tonnes
Tractive effort	20,130 lb	9131 kg

Built 1943

1950   Beyer Garratt Class   4-8-2 + 2-8-4

The most powerful steam locomotives ever used on the Q.R. carried no other classification than "Beyer Garratt".

Final big power of the 1950s, the 4-8-2 + 2-8-4 Beyer Garratt.

169

Despite the misadventures of the ASG project during World War II, the department went ahead with an order for 30 articulateds—10 from Beyer, Peacock, and 20 by an associated builder, Franco-Belge of France. The fine red locos arrived in 1950 and were used initially on passenger and freight trains based at Rockhampton, but soon they appeared more widely throughout the system.

Problems were experienced with claims of excessive heat conditions for enginemen in tunnels, and to some extent operations were restricted.

The advent of diesel power meant their concentration on heavy export coal traffic in the Dawson Valley, which was to be the last major task for the Beyer Garratts—in all a short working life.

They were removed from the register between 1964 and 1970 and one (No. 1009) is on view at Redbank Museum.

Principal dimensions

Driving wheels	4 ft 3 in	1295 mm
Cylinders (4)	$13\frac{3}{4} \times 26$ in	337×660 mm
Pressure	200 lb	1379 kPa
Weight	137 tons	139.2 tonnes
Tractive effort	32,770 lb	14 864 kg

Built 1950

TANK AND MISCELLANEOUS TYPES

1948   DD17 Class   4-6-4T

The Q.R. was always "big" in suburban tank engines, beginning with the locally designed 6D16 (4-6-2T, later 4-6-4T) of 1905 and followed by the D17 of 1924. Brisbane services imposed a strain on keeping these veterans from wearing out, so that additional loco-

The 6D16, first Q.R. loco to employ a 12-ton (12.2-tonne) axle load.

motives became a pressing need for commuter traffic.

Using the basis of the D17 class, and drawing on some AC16 features, a design was completed for a modernized and efficient suburban engine, which was built by Ipswich Workshops in 1948. The 12 locos were

D17 No. 47 was typical of the suburban 4-6-4Ts operating out of Brisbane Central.

DD17 of 1948, the Q.R.'s final suburban tank design.

classed DD17 and painted a lighter shade of blue. Improvements included superheaters, self-cleaning smokeboxes and mechanical lubricators.

Soon the nifty machines demonstrated that they could handle the fast short-stop operations without any trouble. Their territory was mostly on northside suburban runs, although they were later moved to transfer and shunting duties as more diesel power arrived for the commuter services. They were written off between 1966 and 1969. Four have been preserved. One (1051) is at the Redbank Rail Museum while three (1046, 1047 and 1049) provide motive power for the Zig Zag Railway near Lithgow, N.S.W.

Principal dimensions
Driving wheels	4 ft 3 in	1295 mm
Cylinders	17 × 24 in	432 × 610 mm
Pressure	180 lb	1241 kPa
Weight	62 tons	63 tonnes
Tractive effort	20,810 lb	9 439 kg

Built 1948–52

Narrow gauge 610 mm (2 ft)

1924   B9½ Class   0-6-2

The Q.R. operated its own "narrow gauge" at Innisfail, where 48 km (30 miles) of 610-mm (2-ft) gauge had been taken over from regional authorities in 1914.

Thirteen steam locomotives were used in the sugar and mixed traffic at various times, the largest being three John Fowler B9½ tender type. The small 0-6-2s were capable of moving prodigious loads on the fairly level tracks, and worked without incident for many years until they were displaced by locally built diesel-hydraulics in 1961–2.

The B9½-class Fowler 0-6-2 working the Innisfail cane tramway.

The last of the B9½ class (No. 11) has been preserved in Fitzgerald Park, Innisfail.

Principal dimensions
Driving wheels	2 ft 4 in	711 mm
Cylinders	9½ × 14 in	241 × 356 mm
Pressure	160 lb	1103 kPa
Weight	22½ tons	22.9 tonnes
Tractive effort	5,776 lb	2620 kg

Built 1924

WESTERN AUSTRALIAN GOVERNMENT RAILWAYS 1879

Western Australia's first steam railways were two south-western logging lines, the 19-km (12-mile) Lockville–Yoganup tramway of 1871 and the 40-km (25-mile) track from Rockingham to Jarrahdale in 1872. Late in commencing its own railway enterprise, the government studied the merits of an even narrower 914-mm (3-ft) gauge before opting for the same width as the narrow-gauge eastern systems. By the early 1890s, W.A.G.R. tentacles were stretching out, one of the longest main lines extending 612 km (380 miles) towards the boom towns of Coolgardie and Kalgoorlie on the Eastern Goldfields.

Quite substantial land-grant companies played an important role alongside the W.A.G.R. in opening up empty territory in what became Australia's largest State. The 400-km (249-mile) Great Southern Railway Co. was purchased by the government for £1.1 million in 1896. The larger 440-km (273-mile) Midland Railway Co. running from Perth's outskirts to Walkaway near Geraldton continued a separate existence, with quite an individual steam-locomotive stock, right through to the 1950s.

From a distance, W.A.G.R. motive-power policy might appear to adhere closely to the traditions of the smallish colonial engines that British makers in vast numbers sent abroad. To designate them as possibly more "English", W.A.G.R., like Tasmania, kept to the vacuum ejector brake rather than the Westinghouse of other railways. Certainly Kitson, Neilson, Avonside and Beyer, Peacock were builders' names to be

Fairlie 2-4-4-2, from Avonside Engineering Co., introduced on the W.A.G.R. in 1879.

found on those early machines. Yet a closer look at the State's engine development shows an emergence of interesting Baldwin E and C-class Pacifics in the early 1900s—narrow-fireboxed engines that were forerunners of many notable 4-6-2s with wider grate area to consume Collie coal. In all, 197 new locos were introduced from 1900 to 1913.

The stable of light Beyer Garratts, engines of a very "home grown" appearance, commenced with the M and Ms classes of 1911–13, to be followed in 1930 by the W.A.G.R.'s own Msa, which is reputedly the first Garratt type constructed in the southern hemisphere. During World War II, the W.A.G.R.'s articulated experience was to provide much of the design basis of the Commonwealth Land Transport Board's emergency Australian Standard Garratt (ASG), some of which were built in the State workshops, others at Newport, Islington and the Clyde Co. For a variety of reasons, not all of them due to the locomotive itself, the ASG history is less than auspicious, and the 57 Garratts completed came to a relatively early end.

From the department's Midland Workshops an effective line of engine power began to appear from the 1920s on, of which the best known is probably the P/Pr family of express and mixed-traffic Pacifics, and J. W. Broadfoot's surprising S Mountain type of

1943 which raised maximum non-articulated tractive effort in the West to a respectable 13 925 kg (30,700 lb).

Arrival in 1946 of British Munitions' trim U-class oil-burners, originally intended for the Sudan, added interest to W.A.G.R. operations; as late as 1967 one of the Pacifics reappeared as a Ut-class tank (4-6-4T). As with Queensland, tank loco design was a particular forte of the West, not only for Perth tracks but operating into nearer rural areas as well. But perish the thought of two locomotive branches talking together — the tank engines of Brisbane and W.A.G.R. to the end of their days remained as dissimilar as the proverbial chalk and cheese.

In the trail of the U class, British builds appeared in numbers: the North British Pm and Pmr (roller bearing) "improved" Pacifics, the 60 Beyer, Peacock 4-8-2s of 1951–2 and, finally, the V class 2-8-2 from Robert Stephenson and Hawthorns Ltd in 1955–6, a 136.1-tonne (134-ton) heavy freight type with power reverse, thermic syphons, roller bearings — surely one of the most impressive steam horses to appear on narrow gauge anywhere.

Gauge 1067 mm (3 ft 6 in)

PASSENGER TYPE

1902   Es Class   4-6-2

While the title of world's first Pacific-type locomotive probably should be awarded to the lone and lesser known "Jubilee" of 1897, delivered by Baldwin to Millar's Timber and Trading Co., Western Australia, the accolade for pioneering the Pacific usually goes to the New Zealand Railways and their Baldwin 4-6-2s of 1901.

One of the world's early Pacifics, the Es class in Perth.

At the same time as that other 1067-mm (3 ft 6 in) government system across the Tasman Sea awaited its engines, the W.A.G.R. had also launched into the Pacific design with an Ec-class Baldwin compound of 1901, followed in 1902 by the British-built E class for main-line passenger trains. Three builders—Nasmyth Wilson, Vulcan Foundry and North British—contributed to the stable of 65 locos which were later upgraded to Es class through the adoption of superheating. During later years the cylinder diameter was increased from 432 mm (17 in) to 457 mm (18 in) on 21 locos and to 483 mm (19 in) on another seven.

Gradually the Es was overtaken by larger power of the P Pacific type, and all were written off in 1963. Worth noting is that the two-wheel truck beneath the Es firebox was employed for the purpose of weight distribution, and it was not until the arrival of the P in the mid-1920s that advantage was taken of the Pacific design to accommodate a wider grate.

One Es (No. 308) has been retained at Bassendean Museum.

Principal dimensions

Driving wheels	4 ft 6 in	1372 mm
Cylinders	19 × 23 in	483 × 584 mm
Pressure	160 lb	1103 kPa
Weight	84½ tons	85.9 tonnes
Tractive effort	20,910 lb	9485 kg

Built 1902–12

1924   P/Pr/Pm/Pmr Class   4-6-2

In 1924 the W.A.G.R. introduced the first 10 P-class Pacifics, which proved to be among the system's most successful locomotives. Unlike the West's earlier 4-6-2s, these were the first to incorporate a wide firebox over the trailing truck. The design was adapted for a further three derivative classes, with deliveries extending over the next 26 years.

The P class were built by North British for passenger express work, while the W.A.G.R. contributed a further 15 from Midland Workshops in 1927–9. In 1938 Midland produced another 10 locomotives based on the P class but carrying a higher boiler

The P of 1924 commenced a Pacific stable that lasted through to the Pmr of 1950.

pressure and classified as Pr; eight P class were later converted to Pr.

The Pr became the system's main passenger express locomotives, and carried the names of State rivers. After the 1939–45 war, North British supplied a further 35 locomotives which were a modernized version of the Pr. They arrived in 1950 with modifications that included a Cartazzi trailing truck, power reverse and mechanical lubrication of the coupled axle boxes; classification was Pm. While under construction, 16 of these locomotives were equipped with roller bearings on the coupled axles and entered service as the Pmr.

Pmr 733 carrying a country train headboard of the steam era.

Replaced by diesel power, the Pacifics were withdrawn by 1971. One P class (508), one Pr (521) and one Pm (701) have been preserved at the Bassendean Museum. Three Pmr class are on display in country towns as follows: Coolgardie (729), Kalgoorlie (715) and Northam (721).

Principal dimensions

Driving wheels	4 ft 6 in	1372 mm
Cylinders	19 × 26 in	483 × 660 mm
Pressure	175 lb	1207 kPa
Weight	102½ tons	104 tonnes
Pm/Pmr	109 tons	110.7 tonnes
Tractive effort	25,855 lb	11 728 kg

Built 1924–50

1946/1956   U/Ut Class   4-6-2/4-6-4T

Chronic motive-power shortages existed throughout Australia after World War II. In these difficult circumstances Western Australia was quick to take up portion of a surplus order for 4-6-2 tender locomotives which had been intended for North Africa. They were North British machines constructed to requirements of the British Ministry of Munitions, and were delivered in 1946–7 as the oil-burning U class.

As Pacific types familiar to the W.A.G.R. the 14 class members handled express trains until the arrival

Pacific with a difference: ex-British Ministry of Munitions oil-burning U class.

of the first diesel-electric main-liners. The Us were transferred to freight working in the 1950s and then withdrawn as boiler renewals fell due.

One member (664) had been altered to burn coal in 1954; in 1956 it underwent further major surgery, being converted back to oil fuel as a 4-6-4T for suburban services and classified Ut. Though laid aside in 1959, two years later the Ut and the five U-class were returned to service during a serious coal shortage. After about five months they were withdrawn again, except for running a few enthusiast and freight specials. Scrapping took place in 1970, except for U class 655 and the sole Ut class, which have been preserved at Bassendean.

It should be recalled that the sprightly U class permitted the introduction in November 1947 of the Australind express, running the 185 km (115 miles) from Perth to Bunbury in $3\frac{1}{4}$ hours, which was the fastest narrow gauge passenger schedule in Australia.

Beneath that chunky tank lurks a British-made U class—the lone Ut conversion of 1957.

Principal dimensions

Driving wheels	4 ft 6 in	1372 mm
Cylinders	18 × 24 in	457 × 610 mm
Pressure	180 lb	1241 kPa
Weight	107¾ tons	109.5 tonnes
Ut	80 tons	81.3 tonnes
Tractive effort	22,032 lb	9994 kg

Built 1946–7 (Ut 1956)

GOODS TYPE

1881 A Class 2-6-0

Among the motive power purchased by the W.A.G.R. for the first section of the Eastern line were nine 2-6-0s similar to the South Australian Railways' W class (see p. 118).

Three contractors' engines of similar design were added to the fleet. The A class, built by Beyer, Peacock, were used on light branch lines and shunting and jetty duties. Several were sold to timber companies; the first was withdrawn in 1939 but most of the remainder stayed in service until the 1950s.

"Edward Keane", contractor's engine of 1876, later absorbed into the A class.

A class 11, withdrawn in 1955, was displayed at the South Perth Zoo and in 1969 transferred to Bassendean; another (No. 15) has been preserved at Bunbury.

Principal dimensions

Driving wheels	3 ft 3 in	991 mm
Cylinders	12 × 20 in	305 × 508 mm
Pressure	120 lb	827 kPa
Weight	29½ tons	30 tonnes
Tractive effort	7,090 lb	3216 kg

Built 1881–5

1889   G Class   2-6-0 & 4-6-0

Two sets of wheel arrangement are covered by W.A.G.R.'s G classification. One, a 2-6-0, dates back to 1889, when the first of 48 mixed-traffic engines were imported. Identical locomotives to the same versatile design were acquired by other Australian 1067-mm (3 ft 6 in) gauge systems (i.e., S.A.R.'s Y and T.G.R.'s C classes).

The design was developed by Beyer, Peacock although the W.A. versions came from Dubs & Co. The G class was ideal for handling substantial loads at low speeds over light and indifferent track; 48 were in service in 1899. However, the two-wheel leading truck made the engines unsuitable for passenger operations and in 1895 the W.A.G.R. acquired the first of 23 similar locomotives with a four-wheel bogie. Being otherwise identical, these 4-6-0s were grouped with the G class.

During World War II, 13 G-class 2-6-0s were sold to the Commonwealth Railways, where they were known as the NFC class; some of these were later returned to the W.A.G.R. The C.R. also acquired 13 of the 4-6-0 type.

A steam survivor—G233, the "Leschenault Lady" of Bunbury tourist trains.

Two of the G class remain in service operating the "Leschenault Lady" tourist service out of Bunbury—4-6-0 No. 123 and 2-6-0 No. 233. Another 4-6-0 (118) has been preserved at Kalamundra and a 2-6-0 (71) is at Yarloop.

Principal dimensions

Driving wheels	3 ft 3 in	991 mm
Cylinders	$14\frac{1}{2} \times 20$ in	368×508 mm
Pressure	160 lb	1103 kPa
Weight	42 tons	42.7 tonnes
4-6-0	48 tons	48.8 tonnes
Tractive effort	13,626 lb	6181 kg
4-6-0	11,497 lb	5125 kg

Built 1889–97

1896 O Class 2-8-0

Rather like a centipede type, the O was purchased in the late 1890s for main-line freight. The 46 locomotives in the class were a larger version of the 4-6-0 Gs. They were displaced by the bigger F-class 4-8-0s, but continued an active life on country branches. Ten were converted to N-class tanks in 1907–8.

The "Long Tom" look of the consolidation O class.

Surplus equipment from the rebuild was used in the construction at Midland Workshops of the Oa class, 10 locos which were generally similar to the O-class design but with larger driving wheels. Dubs O-class No. 218 is on display at Bassendean.

Principal dimensions

Driving wheels	4 ft $1\frac{1}{2}$ in	1257 mm
Cylinders	$15\frac{1}{2} \times 21$ in	394×533 mm
Pressure	160 lb	1103 kPa
Weight	63 tons	64 tonnes
Tractive effort	13,040 lb	5915 kg

Built 1896–8

1902   Fs Class   4-8-0

The West's "big power" buying spree of the early 1900s included 4-8-0s for main-line freight working, known as the F class. Following the original 15, by 1913 another 57 locos had been added from Dubs and North British. During the 1920s the whole of the class was fitted with bigger cylinders and superheaters and classified "Fs". All were withdrawn by the late 1950s. No. 460 has been preserved at the Bassendean Museum.

The Fs twelve-wheeler, later superheated, from the "new engine" programme of 1902.

Principal dimensions

Driving wheels	3 ft 6½ in	1079 mm
Cylinders	19 × 23 in	483 × 584 mm
Pressure	175 lb	1207 kPa
Weight	85½ tons	86.9 tonnes
Tractive effort	23,264 lb	10 552 kg

Built 1902–14

1912 M/Ms/Msa Class   2-6-0 + 0-6-2

The Western Australian Government Railways took to the Garratt locomotive surprisingly early in the life of the then remarkably new Beyer design. The first Garratt was acquired in 1912, only three years after the midget K-class pioneers had appeared on the Tasmanian narrow gauge; built to the 2-6-0 + 0-6-2 wheel arrangement, these were classified M and employed on light-line passenger operations. Beyer, Peacock supplied a further seven engines in 1913–14 with the improvement of superheating, which resulted in the classification of Ms.

Among the world's earliest Beyer Garratts, the Ma (later M) class of 1912.

The Garratts continued to prove so successful that in 1930 the W.A.G.R. turned to producing similar engines of its own, the Msa—first Garratt-type to be built in Australia and, reputedly, first originating in the southern hemisphere. The improved Garratts, with a higher tractive effort, were used on light tracks, including the hilly portions of the south-western corner, where they were rostered on mixed and freight traffic. Though the earlier engines had been withdrawn

By 1930 the Msa Garratt was the West's third articulated type.

in the late 1940s, the Msa continued through to the 1960s.

The various "Ms" represented a significant link in the development of a light Garratt on 1067-mm (3 ft 6 in) rails, yet the whole type was scrapped.

Principal dimensions

Driving wheels	3 ft 3 in	991 mm
Cylinders	13¼ × 20 in	337 × 508 mm
Pressure	175 lb	1207 kPa
Weight	74 tons	75.2 tonnes
Tractive effort	26,784 lb	12 149 kg

Built 1913–30

1943   ASG Class   4-8-2 + 2-8-4

Who today remembers the Commonwealth Land Transport Board? This was the wartime organization that authorized the construction of 65 Garratt locomotives to an untried design featuring low axle load and relatively high haulage ability. Faced with bottlenecks on all 1067-mm (3 ft 6 in) gauge systems and the reality of the Japanese threat to the north, the Board adopted a Western Australian concept for the Garratt and urgent orders were placed with Newport Workshops for 16, Islington Workshops for 12, Clyde Engineering Co. for 27 and Midland Workshops

A World War II design, the ASG served on all government narrow gauges and two private lines.

(W.A.) for 10. The first engine was built in four months. Yet, when 57 were completed by December 1945, construction of further ASGs was cancelled.

Although the basic plan appeared sound, the ASGs (i.e., Australian Standard Garratt) were plagued with mishaps and controversy wherever they were used on government systems. Allocated to the Queensland, Western Australian and Tasmanian systems, they were the subject of black bans by loco crews and, in Western Australia, a Royal Commission. Only in Tasmania were they relatively successful, and then only after substantial modifications.

One ASG was sold to the Australian Portland Cement Co. for its Fyansford quarry operation near Geelong, Vic. The Emu Bay Railway Co. of Tasmania operated five ASGs in the 1950s on freight, ore and even passenger trains. Of the bulk of the engines one never turned a wheel, several ran for only two months and most were withdrawn after a few years.

The South Australian Railways used six ASGs as stop-gap motive power on the Port Pirie–Broken

Hill line in 1952 while awaiting arrival of the 400-class Beyer Garratts.

The Emu Bay ASGs were last in service, and these finished up as the diesels were introduced in the early 1960s.

The former Fyansford ASG has been preserved and the owners of No. G33, Geelong Steam Preservation Society, hope to steam it.

Principal dimensions

Driving wheels	4 ft 0 in	1219 mm
Cylinders (4)	14½ × 24 in	368 × 610 mm
Pressure	200 lb	1379 kPa
Weight	119 tons	120.9 tonnes
Tractive effort	34,520 lb	15 658 kg

Built 1943–5

1943 S Class 4-8-2

Plans to develop a mixed-traffic locomotive during the 1930s did not eventuate until 1943 when Midland Workshops rolled out the first of ten new S class. They were tried on passenger and freight services on the Eastern Goldfields line, and later they saw service on the South-West. As built, these smart 4-8-2s had a semi-streamlined cowling along the boiler top, of

"Bruce", Midland Shops No. 541, an S class with abbreviated boiler trunking.

which the rear half was eventually removed. A reduction in coal capacity lifted the tender water space and gave the locos a wider availability. Named after mountains in Western Australia, they continued in service until the last days of steam in late 1971. No. 549 has been retained for display at the Bassendean Museum. Another S class is on display in Perth Station.

Principal dimensions

Driving wheels	4 ft 0 in	1219 mm
Cylinders	19 × 24 in	483 × 610 mm
Pressure	200 lb	1379 kPa
Weight	119 tons	120.9 tonnes
Tractive effort	30,685 lb	13 918 kg

Built 1943–7

1951   W Class   4-8-2

Part of the final steam modernization programme, the 60 W class proved very effective machines in freight and passenger duties. Designed and built by Beyer, Peacock in 1951–2, they handled big loads at speed and were popular with crews for their riding characteristics, power reverse equipment and roller-bearing axleboxes. The same design was adopted by the Silverton Tramway Co. for their four semi-streamlined locomotives, also known as W class.

The W.A.G.R. machines continued in service long after the diesels appeared, and the first withdrawals were not made until 1970. Within several years, however, virtually all the class had been scrapped except that several were retained for display and operation. Two (933, 934) were purchased by the Pichi Richi Railway Co. for running in South Australia, while a third (916) was acquired for spare parts. No. 953 has been preserved at the Bassendean

Like other modern locos, the Mountain-type W arrived as the steam era declined.

Museum and Nos 920, 903 and 945 have been acquired by a steam preservation group for operating at Pinjarra, W.A. Two are also on display in country towns—Albany (947) and Esperance (919).

Principal dimensions

Driving wheels	4 ft 0 in	1219 mm
Cylinders	16 × 24 in	406 × 610 mm
Pressure	200 lb	1379 kPa
Weight	101 tons	102.6 tonnes
Tractive effort	21,760 lb	9870 kg

Built 1951–2

1955 V Class 2-8-2

In the very swansong of steam, the W.A.G.R.'s

Mikado V-class No. 1223, last and most impressive locos in the twilight of steam.

massive V-class locomotives were unloaded at Fremantle docks in 1955–6. C. W. Clarke, Assistant Commissioner (Engineering) set the specifications for the 24 engines.

Built to a Beyer, Peacock design by Robert Stephenson & Hawthorn Ltd for heavy coal haulage, they were equipped with roller bearings, thermic syphons and power reverse. These impressive locos gave excellent service, at first on coal trains and later on heavy freights along the Great Southern and South-West routes. The last V was officially retired on Christmas Eve 1971. Fortunately three have been retained for display. One (1220) is at Bassendean Museum, another (1223) at Midland Workshops and a third (1215) at Collie.

Principal dimensions

Driving wheels	4 ft 3 in	1295 mm
Cylinders	19 × 26 in	483 × 660 mm
Pressure	215 lb	1482 kPa
Weight	134½ tons	136.7 tonnes
Tractive effort	33,633 lb	15 256 kg

Built 1955–6

TANK AND MISCELLANEOUS TYPES

1880 C Class 0-6-0ST

Two 0-6-0 saddle tanks were on hand in 1880 for the opening of the first section of the Eastern line between Fremantle and Guildford—also the first railway in Perth. These were built to a conventional design by Robert Stephenson & Co. of England, who was also to produce the W.A.G.R.'s last steam locos.

In 1888 small four-wheel tenders were added although the saddle tanks remained, and about this time they were listed as C class and numbered 1 and 2. In 1900 C1 was sold to a timber company in the south-west of the State, to operate under the names of "Kitty" or "Katie". In 1956 "Katie" was retired from active service, but later the W.A.G.R. acquired it for

"Katie", saddle tank No. 1 of W.A.G.R. C class.

preservation. The historic loco is displayed at the Bassendean Transport Museum.

Principal dimensions
Driving wheels   3 ft 0 in   914 mm

Cylinders	10 × 18 in	254 × 457 mm
Pressure	120 lb	827 kPa
Weight	25½ tons	25.9 tonnes
Tractive effort	4,960 lb	2250 kg

Built 1880

1889   H Class   0-6-0T

Two small tank locomotives were delivered in 1889–90 for use on the then isolated Bunbury–Boyanup line. One of these, No. 18, was sold to the Public Works Department in 1911 and remained at Bunbury for 40 years; the other, No. 22, was shipped to Port Hedland where it operated on the Marble Bar line until closure in 1951. No 18 is now at Bassendean.

Principal dimensions

Driving wheels	2 ft 3 in	686 mm
Cylinders	9 × 14 in	229 × 356 mm
Pressure	120 lb	827 kPa
Weight	14 tons	14.2 tonnes
Tractive effort	4,032 lb	1829 kg

Built 1889–90

1896   N Class   4-4-4T

These tank locomotives with the unusual wheel arrangement (at least for Australian narrow gauge) were intended as medium power for Perth suburban services. Neilson & Co. delivered the first five in 1896 and next year an order was placed with Robert Stephenson & Co. for a further 12 for suburban operations in the booming goldfields city of Kalgoorlie. By 1901 an additional 15, making 32 in all, had been supplied from Nasmyth Wilson and Co.

Unique among suburban tanks, the N with 4-4-4 wheel arrangement.

Although passenger services declined in Kalgoorlie, Perth traffic flourished and the N class was again expanded by 10 conversions from 2-8-0 tender locomotives.

Though the engines continued to run throughout the difficult period of World War II, they were displaced soon afterwards by larger tank locomotives. By 1961 only two N class remained. The last engine, 201, has been preserved at the Bassendean Museum.

Principal dimensions
Driving wheels   4 ft 0 in   1219 mm

Cylinders	15½ × 21 in	394 × 533 mm
Pressure	160 lb	1103 kPa
Weight	44 tons	44.7 tonnes
Tractive effort	13,454 lb	6103 kg

Built 1896–1908

1946　Dd Class　4-6-4T

At the end of World War II when a number of E-class 4-6-2 tender-type had reached major overhaul, eight were used in the construction of 4-6-4T (tank) locomotives to relieve the pressure on suburban services; they were classified Dm. The alteration proved so satisfactory that next year Midland Workshops built an additional 10 locos to the same "Baltic" wheel arrangement, under the direction of C. M. E. Mills who, incidentally, had supervised the ASG design.

Though built for Perth commuters, the 4-6-4T Dm and Dds sometimes worked to nearer country centres.

Known as the Dd, the latter class, though intended for suburban runs, were also found on short country journeys when tender engines were not available. Diesel railcars edged the tanks off suburban runs in the 1950s although the Dd and Dm classes continued in peak-hour passenger as well as freight traffic for another 10 years. Half the Dd class were withdrawn in 1968 and the others continued as shunters until 1971. Dd-class 592 was used for enthusiast specials until presentation to the Bassendean Museum.

Principal dimensions

Driving wheels	4 ft 6 in	1372 mm
Cylinders	18 × 23 in	457 × 584 mm
Pressure	160 lb	1103 kPa
Weight	72½ tons	73.7 tonnes
Tractive effort	18,768 lb	8513 kg

Built 1946

PRIVATE RAILWAYS

In the late 1970s, long after steam locomotives had been scrapped from the government railways, one could drive down a street in the rich Hunter Valley region of New South Wales and suddenly come upon a heavy 2-8-2 tank going about its business on a string of loaded coal wagons; it was as if, for steam, nothing had ever changed. Here among mine dumps, poppet heads and velvety green fields was the last stronghold of the steam engine—the South Maitland Railway Company, heading west from East Greta on the N.S.W. Northern line and, but a few kilometres below it, the former J. & A. Brown railway to Richmond Vale, once the haunt of Great Central type 2-8-0s and the fascinating Mersey tanks from the line that ran between Liverpool and Birkenhead.

Fortunately the N.S.W. coalfields were uniquely

Coals to Newcastle: the S.M.R.'s line in the Hunter Valley.

placed to sustain steam in a hostile diesel age. Not so lucky were the many steam locomotives of Australia's other private railways, some of them quite considerable in size and traffic, such as the 446-km (277-mile) Midland Company of Western Australia and the strategically placed Silverton Tramway of the N.S.W.–S.A. border which used the handsome W Mountain class on heavy ore trains.

Rapid growth has occurred in the number of private railways that today serve the immense iron-ore and other mineral projects of Australia's far north and western corners. None of these railways has ever carried steam, the more conventional motive power being large American-style diesel-electrics of up to 3600 hp, with trailing loads of 24 000 tonnes (23 622 tons).

Yet steam will still make itself heard in the remote Pilbara, in the shape of no less than an historic G.W.R.

Famous G.W.R. ten-wheeler, "Pendennis Castle", now on the Hamersley iron ore railway.

Castle class 4-6-0, "Pendennis Castle", purchased and brought to Australia from England by local fans who want to operate it again on the rails of Hamersley Iron. Among the surviving private systems, the largest is the now all-diesel Emu Bay Railway Co., threading through spectacular mountain and dense bushland scenery. This is a line that once boasted 4-8-2 + 2-8-4 Beyer Garratts and blue-painted 4-8-0 Dubs that in winter would plough through snowstorms on the 136-km (85-mile) narrow gauge to Tasmania's wild West Coast.

Once Australia's largest narrow-gauge locos, the E.B.R.'s Beyer Garratts.

SOUTH MAITLAND RAILWAYS
Gauge 1435 mm (4 ft 8½ in)

1912   10 Class   2-8-2

In order to have the same load rating as N.S.W. standard goods locomotives, with which they interchanged, the East Greta Coal Mining Co. (later to become South Maitland Railways) ordered some quite unusual tank locomotives from Beyer, Peacock. They have the same basic design as the 50-class 2-8-0s, with side tanks and bunker added in place of tender. The altered wheel arrangement is 2-8-2.

What diesel age? S.M.R.'s 10-class tank alive and steaming outside East Greta depot.

Although fitted with a saturated boiler, the locomotives steam well, run smoothly and perform without trouble on the "conveyor belt" operation between East Greta Junction and the various collieries served by the line. A total of 14 were built, all by Beyer, Peacock, between 1912 and 1925—although some were withdrawn in 1967. Coal traffic boomed again and all were returned to service, some with new boilers and rebuilt frames. Several have also been used on the former J. & A. Brown lines from Pelaw Main to Hexham. It seems that the ease and cheapness of obtaining coal for the 10 class has so far defeated the diesels. All are still in service on Australia's oldest surviving steam railway.

Principal dimensions

Driving wheels	4 ft 3 in	1295 mm
Cylinders	20 × 26 in	508 × 660 mm
Pressure	180 lb	1241 kPa
Weight	83 tons	84.3 tonnes
Tractive effort	29,365 lb	13 320 kg

Built 1912–25

J. & A. BROWN
Gauge 1435 mm (4 ft 8½ in)

1907 Mersey Tank 0-6-4T

The Mersey tank, which began by spending half its running life in the dark, was a most unlikely machine to appear in Australia. Colliery magnate John Brown, never one to waste a dime, bought the engines going cheap as a replacement for some of his iron-horse veterans on the Richmond Vale colliery railway, out of Hexham near Newcastle. Beyer, Peacock, the builders of the 1885-style inside-cylinder tanks, removed the condenser and smoke-suppression equipment which had been employed on the U.K. line between Liverpool and Birkenhead through the Mersey tunnels, before the tanks were shipped to Australia. First to arrive was No. 5, "The Major" (named after Major Isaac who began the trial bores under the Mersey in 1879); distinguished by outside frames and a rather ungainly 0-6-4 appearance, the 5 was stationed at the shed of the Minmi "ghost railway", and hauled trains from Pelaw Main and Richmond mines.

The Mersey tank, showing outside frames and rods.

Three other Merseys were also purchased, and having operated on the 1-in-27 grades of the now electrified Liverpool track, showed that they contained ample power to move the weighty coal trains; usually they went bunker-first towards Hexham, to allow the footplate crew to escape the worst of the fumes through the John Brown tunnels (did they ever wish the condensing equipment were restored?). A longish, rigid wheelbase, however, did not altogether fit the Merseys for Richmond Vale conditions; they were later downgraded to shunting and when the R.O.Ds arrived in 1924 were mostly laid aside. No. 5 was rescued from the graveyard track in 1973 and now resides at Thirlmere R.T.M.

Principal dimensions

Driving wheels	4 ft 7 in	1372 mm
Cylinders	21 × 26 in	533 × 660 mm
Pressure	150 lb	1034 kPa
Weight	68 tons	69.1 tonnes
Tractive effort	25,017 lb	11 348 kg

Built 1885

1924 R.O.D.

Seeking additional motive power for his extensive colliery railway system between Hexham, Minmi, and Pelaw Main in the Newcastle area, the coal magnate John Brown acquired three R.O.D. locomotives while on a visit to the U.K. During World War I, over 500 of the British Government's Railway Operating Division locos had been built for service in Europe. The type was a repeat of J. G. Robinson's heavy freight 2-8-0s for the Great Central Railway, introduced in 1911.

Those on the J. & A. Brown line were so successful that a further 10 were acquired from surplus U.K.

Far from World War I battlefields, R.O.D. 2-8-0 on the J. & A. Brown railway.

stocks; this buy varied from the first in that the locos were not fitted with superheaters. Of typical British uncluttered appearance, the R.O.D.s worked for more than 40 years on the Richmond Vale railway, until tapering-off of coal production in the area placed them out of service in the late 1960s. Ten were cut up immediately; Nos 20 and 24, purchased by an English preservation group, later went to the Hunter Valley Steam Railway Museum where they are currently stored. A third has been earmarked for preservation by Coal & Allied Limited, the successor to J. & A. Brown, No. 21 at Freeman's Waterholes on the Cessnock road.

Principal dimensions

Driving wheels	4 ft 8 in	1422 mm
Cylinders	21 × 26 in	533 × 660 mm
Pressure	185 lb	1276 kPa
Weight	123 tons	125 tonnes
Tractive effort	30,300 lb	13 744 kg

Built 1918 (ex J. & A. Brown)

SILVERTON TRAMWAY COMPANY LTD
Gauge 1067 mm (3 ft 6 in)

1912   A Class   4-6-0

The Silverton Tramway Co., which provided the rail connection between Broken Hill and the N.S.W.–S.A. border at Cockburn, operated for the first 20 years with quite small locomotives.

In 1912 the company approached Beyer, Peacock to design and build four main-line 4-6-0 type more in keeping with the volume of ore and freight traffic then being handled. These were delivered the same year and were presentable, efficient machines that for 40 years hauled the company's main ore, freight and passenger trains until the arrival of larger locomotives in the early 1950s.

In its active days, Silverton Tramway's A-class ten-wheeler No. 20.

For a number of years until 1953 the South Australian Railways hired two of the Silverton Company's locos. After being used on shunting duties, the A class was written off by 1960.

One (21) has been preserved at the Mile End Rail Museum.

Principal dimensions

Driving wheels	4 ft 3 in	1295 mm
Cylinders	16½ × 22 in	419 × 559 mm
Pressure	185 lb	1276 kPa
Weight	59 tons	60 tonnes
Tractive effort	18,467 lb	8376 kg

Built 1912–15

1951 W Class 4-8-2

A big boost for the Silverton Tramway Company came in 1951 when four green-liveried 4-8-2s were acquired from Beyer, Peacock. They were based on a very successful design which this builder had completed for the Western Australian Government Railways at the same time, but differed from their Western counterparts in having Westinghouse brakes, and

Silverton Tramway's W-class No. 23 at Broken Hill, before standard gauge came through.

also a semi-streamlined cowling along the top of the boiler.

Despite a reputation for efficiency and free steaming, the W class did not enjoy a long life on the S.T.C. tracks, and were retired with the introduction of diesel-electrics in 1961; however one (25) was steamed intermittently for several years to handle rail-fan excursions.

Two have been preserved. No. 25 is at the Mile End Museum, while another (22) is on display at the Puffing Billy Museum at Menzies Creek, Victoria.

Principal dimensions

Driving wheels	4 ft 0 in	1219 mm
Cylinders	16 × 24 in	406 × 610 mm
Pressure	200 lb	1379 kPa
Weight	97½ tons	99.1 tonnes
Tractive effort	21,760 lb	9870 kg

Built 1951

MIDLAND RAILWAY COMPANY OF WESTERN AUSTRALIA, LTD
Gauge 1067 mm (3 ft 6 in)

1912   C Class   4-6-2

One of the most businesslike private railways was the Midland Railway Co. of Western Australia, which obtained a franchise to operate a 446-km (277-mile) line from near Perth to Walkaway (near Geraldton) on the land-grant system.

By the time the company had disposed of the land it acquired, assets had diminished and in the 1950s its operations were incorporated in the government system.

One of the Midland Co.'s most efficient locomotives were its five C-class 4-6-2s which were supplied by

From Australia's longest private line, Midland's C-class Pacific.

Kitson & Co. of England. Despite their British origins, the Pacific class looked decidedly American in appearance with cowcatcher, high-pitched boilers and large-capacity bogie tenders.

The C class gave good service for many years and were superheated in the 1930s; eventually they were replaced on main services by heavier locos and finished their days on less important trains and duties.

They were withdrawn and scrapped during the late 1950s; none were retained for preservation.

Principal dimensions

Driving wheels	4 ft 1 in	1245 mm
Cylinders	16½ × 22 in	419 × 559 mm
Pressure	160 lb	1103 kPa
Weight	77 tons	78.2 tonnes
Tractive effort	16,624 lb	7541 kg

Built 1912

EMU BAY RAILWAY COMPANY LTD
Gauge 1067 mm (3 ft 6 in)

1900   Dubs   4-8-0

The Emu Bay Railway Co., based on Burnie in north-west Tasmania, commenced operations in the 1880s with low-capacity motive power.

In 1900 it acquired four 4-8-0s from Dubs & Co. for ore, freight and passenger haulage over its steeply graded line.

These were hard-working machines and a fifth was supplied in 1911 by North British which had taken

Shades of the Highland Railway, the Dubs 4-8-0 at Burnie.

over the Dubs organization. Known only as "the Dubs", the locos operated for many years and in the early 1960s two were given a coat of smart paint and other external cosmetic improvements for the company's passenger train, the Westcoaster, which had been introduced to develop tourist traffic.

Though replaced by diesel power in 1963, two Dubs have been preserved—No. 6 at the Zeehan School of Mines and No. 8 at Don Junction.

Principal dimensions

Driving wheels	3 ft 9 in	1143 mm
Cylinders	17½ × 22 in	444 × 559 mm
Pressure	175 lb	1207 kPa
Weight	72 tons	73.2 tonnes
Tractive effort	20,960 lb	9507 kg

Built 1900–11

MT LYELL MINING & RAILWAY COMPANY
Gauge 1067 mm (3 ft 6 in)

1896   Abt   0-4-2T

The 35-km (22-mile) line of the Mount Lyell Mining & Railway Co. on the west coast of Tasmania ascended some grades which defied normal forms of rail traction. Built to connect the mining township of Queenstown with the tidewater port of Regatta Point, the route passed through wild mountainous country which contained long sections of 1-in-16 to 1-in-20 grades.

The company overcame the haulage problem by adopting the Abt rack system, named after its inventor, a European engineer. A toothed rack was placed between the running rails to mesh with toothed wheels on the locomotive; the rack wheels were powered by a separate set of cylinders in addition to those for the normal driving wheels.

Dubs & Co. supplied four 0-4-2T locomotives fitted for Abt working in 1896; a fifth was supplied as late as 1938 by the North British Locomotive Co. which had integrated the Dubs operations many years earlier.

The little Abts pulled ore, freight and passenger trains in a noisy spectacular fashion until 1963 when the railway closed in favour of road transport.

Most of the rack locos have been preserved. No. 1

Up the 1-in-16 from Queenstown, an Abt tank battles with the morning mixed for Strahan.

is at the School of Mines at Zeehan (near Regatta Point), No. 2 is at the Transport Museum in Hobart, No. 3 is at the Mt Lyell works in Queenstown and No. 5 is displayed, with the Abt equipment open to inspection, at the Puffing Billy Museum at Menzies Creek (Vic).

Principal dimensions
Driving wheels	3 ft 0 in	914 mm
Cylinders	11½ × 20 in	292 × 508 mm
Pressure	175 lb	1207 kPa
Weight	26 tons	26.4 tonnes
Tractive effort	17,000 lb	7711 kg

Built 1896–1938

BROKEN HILL PROPRIETARY CO. LTD
Gauges 1067 mm (3 ft 6 in); 1435 mm (4 ft 8½ in)

1914   4-6-0

In 1901 the Broken Hill Proprietary Co. Ltd, Australia's largest industrial railway operator, opened an isolated line from Iron Knob in South Australia to Whyalla on Spencer Gulf to carry iron ore. Being a non-government line, it was known as the Iron Knob Tramway; the gauge was 1067 mm (3 ft 6 in).

Two 4-6-0s purchased from Baldwin Locomotive Works in 1914 could handle around 900-tonne (886-ton) trailing loads—a far cry from those of the earlier motive power which had been small 2-6-0 and 2-6-2T types.

Rolling an empty ore train, B.H.P. No. 4 leaves Whyalla.

However, the ten-wheelers did not remain the line's "big" power for long. Two 2-8-2s were obtained in 1921 which could handle loads of 2337 tonnes (2300 tons), and the 4-6-0s were then relegated to shunting and minor duties until the 1960s when diesel-electrics were used on the "Tramway".

One of the 4-6-0s (No. 4) has been preserved at Mile End Rail Museum.

Also typical of B.H.P. engine power once seen at Newcastle Steelworks, N.S.W., is "No. 16", an 0-4-0T built by H. K. Porter & Co., U.S.A., which was later sold to a private gravel line at Emu Plains, N.S.W., before retirement at the Thirlmere Museum.

Principal dimensions (No. 4)

Driving wheels	3 ft 8 in	1118 mm
Cylinders	16 × 22 in	406 × 559 mm
Pressure	150 lb	1034 kPa
Weight	80 tons	81.3 tonnes
Tractive effort	16,300 lb	7394 kg

Built 1914

BROKEN HILL ASSOCIATED SMELTERS PTY LTD
Gauge 1067 mm (3 ft 6 in)

1919   Peronne   0-6-0T

In addition to small, medium and big power steam locomotives acquired by the main Australian systems, quite a variety of quaint little engines were owned by many industrial concerns. These stubby machines spent their days usually puffing up and down a kilometre or so of siding situated within the plant.

Typical users of these locomotives were collieries, steelworks, power stations and a variety of factories.

Generally these industrial locos were of tank design, high-boilered with two or three driving axles. They were usually supplied by one of the numerous British or American builders who specialized in such "off the peg" power.

Typical of these small engines is "Peronne", one of four similar units used by Broken Hill Associated

A B.H.A.S. 0-6-0T shunter, once a familiar sight in Ellen Street, Port Pirie.

Smelters at the Port Pirie works. Built by Andrew Barclay & Co. of Scotland in 1919, they were used for general shunting of ore wagons until displaced by a diesel-hydraulics in 1961. Today "Peronne" is preserved at the Mile End Rail Museum as a classic example of the hundreds of industrial engines which were once used in Australia. Another B.H.A.S. loco, "Pozieres", is displayed at the Puffing Billy Museum, Menzies Creek, Victoria.

Principal dimensions

Driving wheels	3 ft 0 in	914 mm
Cylinders	10 × 18 in	254 × 457 mm
Pressure	160 lb	1103 kPa
Weight	18½ tons	18.8 tonnes
Tractive effort	6800 lb	3084 kg

Built 1919

COMMONWEALTH PORTLAND CEMENT COMPANY, PORTLAND
Gauge 1435 mm (4 ft 8½ in)

One of Australia's smallest industrial railways, but still a stronghold of steam, the Commonwealth Portland Cement line extends 1.5 km (1 mile) from Portland station (on the N.S.W.P.T.C. Mudgee route) to a terminus within the works yard. Three steam locomotives remain on the roster although not all are in regular operation. Two locos are typical 0-6-0T industrial types from Andrew Barclay, No. 3 built in 1911 and No. 5 in 1916. The third loco is ex-N.S.W.R. No. 2605, a Dubs 2-6-2ST, built in 1892. (See 26 class, N.S.W.R./N.S.W.P.T.C.)

MUSEUMS AND ENTHUSIAST LINES

NEW SOUTH WALES

NSW Rail Transport Museum, Thirlmere, 90 km (56 miles) SW of Sydney.
Gauge 1435 mm (4 ft 8½ in).
A large number of N.S.W. Government and private locomotives and rolling stock are displayed and operated here. Steam-powered trains run on the adjacent Picton-Mittagong loop line at certain weekends and holidays. At certain times, steam excursions operate to more distant parts of N.S.W.

In royal blue livery, 3526 at Thirlmere Museum.

Parramatta Park Tramway Museum, Parramatta, 23 km (14 miles) W of Sydney.
Gauge 1435 mm (4 ft 8½ in).
On a short length of track, Baldwin steam tram motor

Baldwin motor 103A and ex-four-wheel tram in Parramatta Park.

No. 103A operates monthly. Two other industrial locomotives are also displayed, including a Vulcan 0-4-0ST which is in running order.

Hunter Valley Steam Railway and Museum.
Gauge 1435 mm (4 ft 8½ in).
This organization has acquired a large number of

Waiting to be called: ex-R.O.D., ex-J. & A. Brown 2-8-0 in storage at the Hunter Valley Museum.

steam locomotives, both government and industrial, as well as various items of rolling stock. The museum is negotiating for an operating site but, in the meanwhile, the locos and carriages are stored on a disused colliery branch in the Newcastle district.

Lithgow Zig Zag Railway, 156 km (97 miles) W of Sydney.
Gauge 1067 mm (3 ft 6 in).
This co-operative organization operates narrow-gauge steam locomotives from Queensland and South Australia over trackage laid on part of the former Great Zig Zag at Lithgow. This is an impressive scenic and historic enterprise which functions at most weekends and public holidays throughout the year.

Far from Brisbane, DD17 tank No. 1046 climbing the Zig Zag.

Broken Hill Rail Museum, 1125 km (699 miles) W of Sydney.
Two former Silverton Tramway (i.e., railway) Co. locomotives and one S.A.R. engine have been preserved at the museum on S.T.C. property at Railwaytown, a suburb of Broken Hill.

Lachlan Vintage Village, Forbes, 480 km (298 miles) W of Sydney.
Several 610-mm (2-ft) cane tramway locomotives have been acquired for use on the "Britannia Tramway" internal 610-mm (2-ft) gauge track at the historic village in nearby Forbes.

Illawarra Light Railway Museum, Albion Park, 100 km (62 miles) S of Sydney.
A number of standard and narrow gauge locomotives and associated equipment from colliery and industrial users are located here for display and limited operation.

Museum of Historic Engines, Goulburn, 220 km (136 miles) SW of Sydney.

Converted tramcars carry the passengers at the Goulburn Steam Museum.

Gauge 610 mm (2 ft).
In addition to a small canefield locomotive, this museum also has a number of very interesting stationary exhibits such as an early beam-type pumping engine.

A short operating track extends along the riverbank to the museum's front gate.

VICTORIA

Newport Rail Museum, North Williamstown, 9 km (5 miles) W of Melbourne.
Gauge 1600 mm (5 ft 3 in).
About 15 former Victorian Railways steam locomotives and other pieces of historic rolling stock are displayed here in static condition. Enthusiast steam specials also operate frequently from Melbourne.

Line-up of V.R. steam locos, H220 in centre, at rail museum, Melbourne.

Puffing Billy narrow gauge, Belgrave, 40 km (25 miles) E of Melbourne.
A regular 762-mm (2 ft 6 in) line from Belgrave to Lakeside, with Na-class steam locos, operating weekends and holidays.

Puffing Billy Museum, Menzies Creek, 48 km (30 miles) E of Melbourne.

Established in conjunction with the Puffing Billy 762-mm (2 ft 6 in) gauge steam line from Belgrave, this museum contains a number of locomotives on display as well as other items of steam and general railway interest.

Puffing Billy approaching Emerald.

Bellarine Peninsula Railway, Queenscliff (formerly at Belmont Common, Geelong)
Gauge 1067 mm (3 ft 6 in).
Steam locomotives from Victoria, South Australia, Queensland and Tasmania have been acquired for

Ex-S.A.R. T class (left) and former Fyansford industrial locos at Belmont Common, Vic.

display and use on an operating line. The organization is re-opening the Queenscliff-Drysdale V.R. track, which it will convert to 1067-mm (3 ft 6 in) gauge.

SOUTH AUSTRALIA

Mile End Rail Museum, Adelaide.
Gauge 1600 mm (5 ft 3 in).
A large number of S.A.R. broad and narrow-gauge locomotives as well as representative engines from the Commonwealth Railways and Silverton Tramway system are displayed statically at this well-laid-out site which is close to the outskirts of the city proper. Steam fan excursions also run from Adelaide.

Pichi Richi Railway, Quorn, 330 km (205 miles) N of Adelaide.
Gauge 1067 mm (3 ft 6 in).
This is a tourist service operating from Quorn through the picturesque Pichi Richi Pass on the old "trans-

Ex-W.A.G.R. W class arriving from Peterborough to operate the Pichi Richi railway.

continental connection", using steam locomotives and rolling stock from Western Australia and South Australia.

AUSTRALIAN CAPITAL TERRITORY

Canberra. The first locomotive to work into Canberra is located on a plinth outside the railway station.

The Commonwealth Government has acquired three other N.S.W. locomotives for display in the A.C.T. and operation on the nearby Goulburn–Bombala line. Steam services run at various intervals.

QUEENSLAND

Redbank Rail Museum, 27 km (17 miles) SW of Brisbane.
Gauge 1067 mm (3 ft 6 in).
Thirteen Q.R. steam locomotives and other items of

Q.R.'s A10 No. 6 at the entrance to the Locomotive Museum, Redbank.

historic rolling stock and equipment are displayed here in non-operating condition. Enthusiast steam specials run on the Q.R. from time to time.

TASMANIA

Tasmanian Transport Museum, Hobart. Several T.G.R. locomotives and one Mt Lyell rack loco are on display.

Don, 290 km (180 miles) N of Hobart.
The Van Diemen Light Railway Society has acquired four industrial-type and one T.G.R. locomotive for preservation.

School of Mines, Zeehan, 290 km (180 miles) W of Hobart.
Four locomotives associated with Tasmanian West-Coast rail operations are displayed.

WESTERN AUSTRALIA

Transport Museum, *Bassendean*, 11 km (7 miles) E of Perth.
A large number of steam locomotives from the State system and timber and industrial tramways are among the exhibits.

Bunbury, 180 km (112 miles) S of Perth.
The local tourist association operates the vintage train "Leschenault Lady" with two G-class steam locomotives.

Hotham Valley Railway, *Pinjarra*, 83 km (61 miles) S of Perth.
Gauge 1067 mm (3 ft 6 in).
The Pinjarra Steam & Hills Railway Preservation Society is developing an operating line at this location and has acquired three W.A.G.R. locomotives.

STEAM FOR AMUSEMENT

Narrow-gauge steam railways maintained by dedicated enthusiasts but operated specifically for the amusement of tourists, or as part of a working museum, are a growing aspect of the preservation of steam. An example is at Timbertown near Wauchope on the N.S.W. mid-north coast, where an early logging mill has been recreated. In this instance the locomotive power is ex-Queensland sugar mills, rather than from the rough bush railways of long ago. Another line, for which locomotives are on site, is planned in the Megalong Valley of the Blue Mountains.

As time goes on, additional narrow-gauge lines may be resurrected with steam or built as new ventures in Queensland, Victoria and Tasmania.

An 0-4-2 Fowler, owned by the Belbin family, is an example of a preserved narrow-gauge canefields loco.

Ex-sugar-cane 0-6-0 "Green Hornet" on the Timbertown line.

DOWN THE TRAMWAY

Minor members of the steam-locomotive roster were those little engines that laboured on Australia's once numerous timber, mineral and construction tramways, and on the canefields of Queensland. Most of these lines are long departed—with the exception of Queensland's many 610-mm (2-ft) gauge mill tramways which continue to function healthily, although diesel-hydraulics have replaced the dinky 0-4-2s and 0-6-0s.

Fortunately a good cross-section of tramway motive power has been retrieved for preservation at various enthusiast museums, and some, as shown in these pages, still operate, raising the echoes with pip-squeak whistles, the bustle of exhaust and the rattle of midget wheels. Other interesting engines, like the Shay-geared that once ran on Victoria's Powelltown Tramway, have sadly been lost. In these final pages we give a glimpse of what steam was like in the days of the tramways.

When private timber lines dotted the south-west—ten-wheeler "Black Butte" with log train from the W.A. forests.

Cane tram at Nambour.

"Wee Georgie Wood" on the 610-mm (2-ft) Tullah Tramway in western Tasmania.

Of little old engines lost in the bush. . . .

OLD STEAM LOCOMOTIVES

Retired, they huddle, side-tracked by a field—
Giants, who hurtled gamely through the night,
Building the mammoth sinews of the land,
Opening vistas—mountain brow and canyon.
Their urgent whistles plumbed the echoing cloud;
Deep-mouthed, their bells, importunately clanging.
Now they crouch in monstrous silence, waiting,
Where mallows, buttercups, and daisies blow
In little winds about the cindered siding.

> *Bertha Wilcox Smith*
> reprinted by courtesy of THE ROTARIAN

APPENDIXES

APPENDIX A

Wheel Classification

Although steam locomotives were classified in different ways by individual railway systems—usually employing numerals or letters of the alphabet or a combination of both—internationally the steam loco is identified by an easy reference to the arrangement of its wheels. Thus a locomotive with a four-wheel leading bogie, six driving wheels and a two-wheel truck beneath the firebox is referred to as "4-6-2" type. This, the "Whyte" method of identification, was further advanced by sometimes associating the wheel arrangement with a country, region or the name of some famous person connected with the introduction or operation of the engine. Thus the 4-6-2 is also popularly known as the "Pacific" type (it was first built for the New Zealand Railways).

The following is a list of wheel arrangements operated on Australian railway systems which appear in this book.

Single driving wheels
2-2-2

Four driving wheels
0-4-0
2-4-0
0-4-2
2-4-2
4-4-0
4-4-2 "Atlantic"
4-4-4

Six driving wheels
0-6-0
2-6-0 "Mogul"
0-6-2
2-6-2 "Prairie"
2-6-4
4-6-0 "ten wheeler"
4-6-2 "Pacific"
4-6-4 "Hudson"
0-6-4
4-6-4T "Baltic"

Eight driving wheels
2-8-0 "Consolidation"
2-8-2 "Mikado" or "Macarthur"
4-8-0 "twelve wheeler"
4-8-2 "Mountain"
2-8-4 "Berkshire"
4-8-4 "Pocono"

Garratt articulated	*Fairlie type*
0-4-0+0-4-0	0-4-4-0
2-6-0+0-6-2	0-6-6-0
2-6-2+2-6-2	2-4-4-2
4-4-2+2-4-4	
4-8-2+2-8-4	
4-8-4+4-8-4	

Tank locomotives follow the same identification pattern with the addition of T after the driving wheels, or ST to indicate saddle tank and WT for well tank.

APPENDIX B

The Loco Builders

The following is a list of the government workshops and companies which built steam locomotives for the Australian railways. In the engine lists throughout this book, each of the builders is mentioned by name although location or nationality is not always given. In this table, the builders are grouped in order of nationality but not necessarily of size or importance to the Australian scene.

All the overseas manufacturers belonged to private industry, whereas in Australia itself both government and company plants contributed to the locomotive rosters. We apologize if the list omits the names of some builders who supplied only very small numbers of engines; likewise this is not an attempt to include all those other manufacturers who specialized in building geared or narrow-gauge tramway equipment.

Australia's association with engine makers goes back to the very early days of railway history; over the years, many of these companies have absorbed others—e.g., Robert Stephenson and Hawthorns Ltd, and North British which incorporated Dubs—so that as time went on the same stamp of expert workmanship has appeared on builders' plates under different titles.

AUSTRALIA

Victoria

Victorian Railways—Railway Workshops, Williamstown
Railway Workshops, Newport
Railway Workshops, Ballarat North
Railway Workshops, Bendigo North

The Melbourne Locomotive & Engineering Works (David Munro & Co.), South Melbourne
Phoenix Foundry Co., Ballarat
Robison Bros., South Melbourne
Robison Bros., Campbell & Sloss, South Melbourne
Thompson & Co. (Castlemaine) Pty Ltd, Castlemaine

New South Wales

N.S.W. Railways (now part of N.S.W. Public Transport Commission)—Eveleigh Locomotive Workshops, Eveleigh (Sydney)
Cardiff Workshops, Cardiff
Atlas Engineering Co., Haymarket, Sydney
Clyde Engineering Co., Granville
Henry Vale, Sydney

Queensland

Queensland Government Railways—Ipswich Railway Workshops
Evans, Anderson & Phelan, South Brisbane
The Phoenix Engineering Co., Ipswich
Walkers Ltd., Maryborough

South Australia

South Australian Railways/Australian National Railways—Islington Railway Workshops, Islington (Adelaide)
James Martin & Co., Gawler
Perry Engineering Co., Adelaide

Western Australia

Western Australian Government Railways—Midland Railway Workshops, Midland Junction (Perth)

UNITED KINGDOM

England

Sir W. G. Armstrong-Whitworth & Co., Newcastle-on-Tyne
Avonside Engine Co., Bristol
Beyer, Peacock & Co., Gorton Foundry, Manchester
James Cross & Co., St Helens
George England & Co., Hatcham Ironworks, London
William Fairbairne of Manchester
John Fowler & Co., Leeds
R. & W. Hawthorn, Forth Bank Works, Newcastle-on-Tyne
Hudswell, Clarke, & Co. Ltd, Railway Foundry, Leeds
Hunslet Engine Co., Leeds
Kerr, Stuart & Co. Ltd, Stoke-on-Trent
Kitson & Co. Ltd, Airedale Foundry, Leeds
Manning Wardle & Co., Leeds
Nasmyth Wilson & Co., Manchester
Slaughter, Grunning & Co., Bristol
Robert Stephenson & Co., Newcastle-on-Tyne
Robert Stephenson & Co. & Hawthorns Ltd, Darlington
Vulcan Foundry Ltd, Newton-le-Willows, Lancashire
Yorkshire Engine Co.

Scotland

Dubs & Co., Queen's Park Works, Glasgow
Neilson & Co., Glasgow (Neilson Reid)
North British Locomotive Co., Glasgow
Sharp Stewart & Co., Glasgow

EUROPE

Krauss & Co., Munich, Germany
Société St Leonard, Liège, Belgium
Société Franco-Belge de Materiel, Raismes, France

UNITED STATES OF AMERICA

The Baldwin Locomotive Works (Burnham, Parry & Williams), Philadelphia, Pennsylvania
Baldwin-Lima-Hamilton Corp., Philadelphia, Pennsylvania
H. K. Porter & Co., Pittsburgh, Pennsylvania
The Rogers Locomotive Works, Paterson, New Jersey
Vulcan Iron Works, Wilkes Barre, Pennsylvania

PHOTOGRAPH SOURCES

Australian National Railways, 126 (above), 129, 133; B. Belbin, 85, 218 (below); G. Belbin, 227 (above); G. Bond collection, 158; John L. Buckland, 8, 112, 117, 131 (below), 135, 201, 206, 209, 210, 213; David Burke, 121, 126 (below), 131 (above), 212; R. M. Carlisle, 221, 223; B. J. Castle, 115; Clyde Engineering Co., 97; R. Currie, 120, 215, 224; Peter Dunbar, 229 (below); Geoff Grant, 38, 222; John Grimwade, 25; La Trobe Library collection, 11, 20, 23; the late A. R. Lyell, 22, 24, 230; S. B. McCarthy, 202; Bruce Macdonald, 220; National Library collection, 1, 16, 99, 128, 138; National Library, H. B. Ballard collection, 49; National Library, P. A. Butler, 9; New South Wales Government Printer, 80 (above); New South Wales Public Transport Commission, 5, 51, 52, 54, 55, 57, 59, 60, 61, 62, 63, 64, 65, 68, 69, 70, 73, 75, 77, 78, 80 (below), 87, 92, 93, 94, 95, 96, 200; New South Wales Rail Transport Museum collection, 14, 66, 76, 88, 90, 148, 169, 189, 205, 207, 218 (above), 219, 225; N.S.W. R.T.M., R. Brown, 58; N.S.W. R.T.M., L. Oberg, 217; N.S.W. R.T.M., B. D. Reynolds, 83, 102, 144; N.S.W. R.T.M., F. C. Saxon, 71, 74, 82, 85, 86; N.S.W. R.T.M., Alan Templeman, 89; D. O'Brien, 199, 203; Queensland Railways, 6, 152, 153, 155, 156, 160 (above), 161, 163, 167; the late Ken Rogers, 21, 151, 157, 160 (below), 164, 166, 168, 171, 172, 173, 229 (above); South Australian State Transport Authority, 103, 104, 105, 106, 107, 108, 109, 111, 113, 114, 118, 123, 134; C. C. Singleton collection, 140; G. W. Stokes, 188, 197; Tasmanian archives, 149; Tasmanian Government Railways, 141, 142,* 145, 146; Timbertown, 227 (below); Victorian Railways, 17, 19, 26, 27, 28, 29, 31, 32, 33, 34, 36, 37, 40, 41, 42, 44, 45, 46, 47; Western Sun, 228; Westrail (Western Australian Government Railways), 175, 177, 178, 179, 180, 181, 182, 184, 185, 186, 187, 190, 192, 193, 194, 195, 196; H. J. Wright, 13.

GLOSSARY

Air pump Steam-driven compressor mounted on locomotive which supplies air to the Westinghouse brake system of engine and train.

Allan straight-link-motion A type of valve gear.

Articulated (n.) Locomotive in which the "engines" (i.e., driving wheels, cylinders, valve gear) are pivoted to operate individually; the articulated principle is used in the Garratt design.

Auto-stoker Mechanical apparatus (usually a steam-driven screw conveyor) for feeding coal from the tender to the firebox; sometimes employed on the largest freight and express passenger locos.

Axle boxes The housing in which axles are carried through the main frame of the locomotive.

Axle loading That share of the total locomotive weight that rests on each axle.

Balloon stack A wide-topped chimney or funnel which contains spark-arresting apparatus; it was particularly used on old wood-burning locomotives.

Belpaire firebox The rectangular-shaped firebox, as distinct from round or "wagon"-topped boiler-firebox combinations.

Bogie tender The locomotive tender carried on two sets of swivelling trucks, usually of four wheels each, but sometimes six-wheel.

Boiler The pressure vessel of the locomotive in which steam is produced from water.

Booster A small two-cylinder steam engine which is mounted on the trailing truck or bogie to function as an auxiliary power unit, usually on heavy freight locomotives.

Builder's plate A small brass plate attached to a locomotive cab or smokebox, giving details of manufacture and year of completion.

Bunker That portion of the loco tender which contains combustion fuel, i.e., coal, oil or wood; also the fuel-carrying section of a tank locomotive located behind the cab.

Coal-fired Fuelled with coal.

Cowcatcher (also "pilot") Metal frame bolted to the buffer beam of a loco to remove obstacles from the track.

Cutaway cab Loco cab with partially open sides, usually with scalloped effect of metal plating (i.e. as distinct from a cab with windows).

Diamond stack A funnel topped with a diamond-shaped housing in which spark-arresting apparatus is contained (see also "Balloon stack").

Diesel Usually refers to a diesel-electric locomotive in which a diesel motor drives an electric generator, which in turn supplies current to a series of traction motors mounted on the bogie axles.

Feed water heater Apparatus mounted on loco boiler in which water is pre-heated before delivery to the boiler.

Gauge Width between the inside of the railhead, e.g. standard gauge is 1435 mm (4 ft 8½ in).

Injector A system of steam and water-combining nozzles which force water from the tender tank into the loco boiler.

Johnson bar (or reverse lever) A lever in the loco cab which controls reverse and valve gear setting (as distinct from a wheel control).

Leading truck The set of small wheels which are positioned ahead of the driving wheels.

Lip Raised front edge of a loco smokestack.

Livery The distinctive marking and/or colour scheme of a locomotive.

Metals The running rails.

Motive power Type of loco traction employed, i.e. steam motive power, diesel motive power, etc.

Oil burner Steam loco burning oil in the firebox instead of coal.

Power reverse Application of compressed air to assist driver in controlling reverse and valve motion setting.

Pressure The maximum steam pressure to which the boiler is set.

Pull-out regulator Driver's regulator (or throttle) which is operated in "pull-out" motion.

Sand dome Housing on top of the boiler which contains sand for feeding to the rails in the event of wheel slip; usually located next to steam dome.

Shunting Moving carriages or wagons, individually or in groups, from track to track for unloading, servicing or to make up a train.

Siderods The "rods" attached to the loco driving wheels, i.e. connecting rods, coupling rods.

Side tanks Water tanks which are carried on each side of the boiler in the "tank" loco arrangement.

Six-coupled Equipped with six driving wheels, i.e. three on each side. A 4-6-0 "ten-wheeler" is six-coupled.

Smokebox The circular portion of a steam loco forward of the boiler proper. Draught is created when exhaust steam passes through the smokebox, merging with combustion gases drawn through the fire tubes from the firebox; exhaust then passes up the chimney.

Smoke deflectors Large metal plates on either side of the smokebox (or placed alongside the funnel) to "lift" steam and smoke clear of the enginemen's view.

Stack The smokestack, funnel or chimney.

Steam dome The housings, usually of semi-circular external finish, on top of the boiler between smokestack and cab, in which steam gathered from the boiler enters the main steam pipe for delivery to the cylinders.

Stephenson inside motion Valve gear situated between the loco frames.

Superheater Series of tubes or "elements" within the boiler fire tubes in which steam is further increased in temperature and "dried" before delivery to the cylinders.

Tank locomotive A locomotive which carries water and combustion fuel on the same frame as the engine itself, i.e. dispensing with the need for a separate tender.

Tender Coupled to the engine, the tender carries the water and combustion fuel (coal, wood, oil) for the firebox.

Thermic syphon Series of water vessels inside the firebox to

Tractive effort The starting haulage capacity of a locomotive computed through a mathematical formula involving cylinder and driving wheel dimensions, etc. The formula used is as follows:

$$\frac{\text{cylinder diameter}^2 \times \text{stroke} \times 85\% \text{ boiler pressure}}{\text{driving wheel diameter}}$$

Note: 85% b.p. is used on superheated locos and 80% value on saturated.

Trailing bogie The four-wheel bogie located behind the driving wheels and beneath the firebox and cab (e.g. on locos of 4-6-4 or 4-8-4 wheel arrangement).

Trailing truck The two-wheel pivoted unit located behind the driving wheels and beneath the firebox (e.g. on locos of 4-4-2, 4-6-2 or 4-8-2 wheel arrangement).

Vacuum brake ejector Device located on the locomotive to exhaust air from the engine and train vacuum brake pipe (i.e. where the vacuum brake is used instead of the Westinghouse system).

Valance Running board with "skirt" extending from cab to smokebox along to boiler sides.

Vauclain compound system A system of employing high and low pressure cylinders in tandem.

Walschaert valve gear System of rods attached to the outside of driving wheels which regulates the setting of valves for the admission and exhaust of steam to and from the cylinders.

Westinghouse brakes The "fail-safe" system of air brakes connected by hoses from the loco compressor to reservoirs and brake valves located throughout the train.

INDEX OF LOCOMOTIVE CLASSES

Australian National Railways: Central Region
(Ex-South Australian Railways)

		page			page
F	4-6-2T	115–6	500	4-8-4	104–5
P	2-4-0T	114–5	520	4-8-4	109–10
Rx	4-6-0	101–2	600	4-6-2	106–7
S	4-4-0	103–4	620	4-6-2	107–9
T	4-8-0	120–2	700	2-8-2	110–13
V	0-4-4T	116–7	710	2-8-2	110–13
W	2-6-0	118–9	720	2-8-4	110–13
Y	2-6-0	119–20	740	2-8-2	110–13
			750	2-8-2	113–4

400   4-8-2 + 2-8-4   122–4

Australian National Railways: Northern Region
(Ex-Commonwealth Railways)

		page			page
C	4-6-0	129–30	NA	0-4-0T	132–3
Ca/Cn	4-6-0	130–2	NJAB	0-4-0T	134–5
G	4-6-0	127–9	NM	4-8-0	135–6

Australian National Railways: Tasmanian Region
(Ex-Tasmanian Government Railways)

		page			page
A	4-4-0	139–40	M	4-4-2 + 2-4-4	140–1
C	2-6-0	143–5			
H	4-8-2	147–8	M/Ma	4-6-2	142–3
K	0-4-0 + 0-4-0	148–9	Q	4-8-2	146–7
			R	4-6-2	141–2
L	2-6-2 + 2-6-2	145–6			

New South Wales Railways

		page			page
AD60	4-8-4 + 4-8-4	82–4	C32	4-6-0	59–60
			C34	4-6-0	61
C30	4-6-4T	91–2	C35	4-6-0	62–3
C30T	4-6-0	66–7	C36	4-6-0	64–5

		page			page
C38	4-6-2	67–9	Z13	4-4-2T	90–1
D50/53/55	2-8-0	76–8	Z17	4-4-0	57–8
D57/58	4-8-2	79–80	Z18	0-6-0T	85–6
D59	2-8-2	81–2	Z19	0-6-0	71–2
E17	0-6-0	70–1	Z20	2-6-4T	87–8
M36	0-4-2	53–4	Z24	2-6-0	75
X10	0-4-0T	84–5	Z25	2-6-0	73–4
X10	2-4-0T	86–7	Z26	2-6-2ST	89–90
X10	0-4-0	92–3	Z27	2-6-0	78–9
X10	0-4-0ST	93–4	Z28/29	2-8-0	72–3
Z12	4-4-0	55–6	Z15/16	4-4-0	56–7

Queensland Railways

		page			page
A10	0-4-2	154–5	B18¼	4-6-2	161–2
A12/14	4-4-0	155–6	BB18¼	4-6-2	162–3
AC16	2-8-2	168–9	C16	4-8-0	164–5
B9½	0-6-2	173	C17	4-8-0	165–6
B13	4-6-0	157–8	C19	4-8-0	166–7
B15 Con	4-6-0	158–9	DD17	4-6-4T	170–2
PB15	4-6-0	159–61	Beyer Garratt		169–70

Victorian Railways

		page			page
A	4-4-0	20–1	H	4-8-4	36–7
A2	4-6-0	23–4	J	2-8-0	38–9
B	2-4-0	18–19	K	2-8-0	33–4
C	2-8-0	31–2	M	4-4-0T	40–1
DD	4-6-0	21–2	N	2-8-2	34–5
D1/D2	4-6-0	21–2	Na	2-6-2T	46–7
D3	4-6-0	21–2	R	4-6-4	27–8
D4	4-6-2T	44–5	S	4-6-2	25–6
E	2-4-2T	41–3	T	0-6-0	28–9
EE	0-6-2T	41–3	V	2-8-0	30–1
F	2-4-2T	39–40	X	2-8-2	35–6
G	2-6-0 +		Y	0-6-0	29–30
	0-6-2	47–8	Z	0-6-0T	43–4

244

Western Australian Government Railways

		page			*page*
A	2-6-0	182–3	M/Ms/	2-6-0 +	
ASG	4-8-2 +		Msa	0-6-2	187–8
	2-8-4	188–90	N	4-4-4T	196–7
C	0-6-0ST	194–5	O	2-8-0	185
Dd	4-6-4T	197–8	P/Pr/Pm/		
Es	4-6-2	176–8	Pmr	4-6-2	178–80
Fs	4-8-0	186	S	4-8-2	190–1
G	2-6-0 and		U	4-6-2	180–2
	4-6-0	183–4	Ut	4-6-4T	180–2
H	0-6-0T	195	V	2-8-2	192–3
			W	4-8-2	191–2

245

GENERAL INDEX

Abt, 211–12
Adelaide Express, 6
Aramac Tramway, 159
Armstrong Whitworth & Co., 100, 105, 106, 110, 236
Atlas Engineering Works, 55, 235
Australian National Railways Commission, 7, 97
Australian Standard Garratt, 7, 121, 124, 143, 175, 188, 189
Avonside Engine Co., 150, 174, 236

"Baby Singer", 93
Baldwin-Lima-Hamilton Corp., 81, 237
Baldwin Locomotive Works, 21, 30, 46, 59, 72, 95, 125, 128, 132, 139, 151, 155, 164, 168, 175, 176, 177, 213, 217, 237
Ballarat North Workshops, 17, 21, 24, 234
Barclay & Co., Andrew, 215
Bassendean Museum, 120, 177, 179, 181, 183, 186, 191, 192, 193, 194, 195, 196, 198, 226
Beaudesert Tramway, 157
Belbin family, 226
Bellarine Peninsula Railway, 122, 143, 160, 190, 222–3
Bendigo Workshops, 17, 21, 25, 234
Beyer, Charles, 55

Beyer Garratt, 7, 12, 82, 83, 138, 139, 140, 148, 153, 169, 170, 175, 190, 201
Beyer, Peacock, 16, 18, 19, 20, 21, 28, 40, 47, 55, 56, 59, 72, 74, 76, 83, 86, 87, 91, 114, 117, 118, 119, 122, 124, 139, 143, 144, 149, 153, 170, 174, 176, 182, 183, 187, 191, 193, 201, 202, 203, 206, 207, 236
"Black Moguls", 75
break-of-gauge, 6–7
Britannia Tramway, 220
Broadfoot, J.W., 175
Broken Hill Associated Smelters Pty Ltd, 214, 215
Broken Hill Proprietary Co. Ltd., 213, 214
Broken Hill Rail Museum, 220
Brown, J. & A., 199, 202, 203, 204
Brownbill, E.E., 24
Brunel, Isambard Kingdom, 99
builders, locomotive, 234–7

Canadian National Railways, 127, 130
Canadian Pacific Railroad, 17
Cardew, Con, 62
Cardiff Workshops, 81, 87, 93, 235
Central Australia Railway, 134, 135, 164, 166
Central Region, 99–124
Central West Express, 68

Cessnock Express, 91
Chillagoe Railway & Mining Co., 159
Clapp, Sir Harold, 18
Clyde Engineering Co., 59, 64, 67, 76, 80, 112, 125, 128, 146, 175, 188, 235
"Coffee pot", 134
Commonwealth Railways, 60, 97, 119, 121, 133, 134, 157, 165, 183, 223
Consolidation, 72, 76, 151, 156, 233
Cross & Co., James, 236

"Dolly", 115
Dubs & Co., 55, 57, 75, 76, 84, 89, 102, 137, 157, 183, 186, 201, 210–11, 234, 236

Emu Bay Railway Co., 144, 189, 190, 210
England & Co., George, 236
Evans, Anderson & Phelan & Co., 151, 156, 158, 164, 235
Eveleigh Works, 59, 61, 62, 64, 67, 73, 77, 80, 81, 91, 235

Fairbairne, William, 236
Fairlie, 151, 233
"Faugh-a-Ballagh", 150
Fitzgerald Park, Innisfail, 173
Fitzgibbon, Abram, 151
Fowler & Co., John, 173, 236
Franco Belge, *see* Société Franco Belge

Garratt, 47, 122, 138, 139, 145, 187, 188, 233. *See also* Beyer Garratt
Geelong & Melbourne Co., 15
Geelong Steam Preservation Society, 160
"Ghan", 136
Goods Motor, 43
Gorton Foundry, 149. *See also* Beyer, Peacock
Goulburn Museum of Historic Engines, 220–1
Great Central Railway, 204
Great Southern Railway Co., 174
Great Western Railway, 62
"grey nurse", 67

Hamersley Iron, 201
Hawthorn, R. & W., 18, 236
Hawthorn Leslie, 84
"Heavy Harry", 1, 5, 36–7
"High Flyers", 56–7
Hobart–Launceston Express, 138
Hobson's Bay Company, 4, 15
Horniblow, H., 152
Hotham Valley Railway, 226
Hudson wheel arrangement, 27
Hudswell, Clarke & Co. Ltd, 236
Hunslet, 137
Hunslet Engine Co., 78, 236
Hunter Valley Steam Rail Museum, 66, 72, 74, 75,

77, 82, 84, 92, 205, 218–9

Illawarra Light Railway Museum, 220
Indian Railways, 143
Inter-Colonial (Melbourne) Express, 101
Ipswich Workshops, 150, 151, 154, 155, 156, 157, 162, 164, 167, 171
Iron Knob Tramway, 213
Islington Workshops, 101, 102, 108, 109, 110, 115, 119, 121, 175, 188, 235

"Jubilee", 176

"Katie", 194
Kerr, Stuart & Co. Ltd, 236
Kitson & Co., 16, 20, 29, 43, 134, 157, 174, 209, 236
Krauss & Co., 236

Lachlan Vintage Village, 66, 77, 92, 220
Lange, Herman, 55
"Leschenault Lady", 184, 226
Lockville–Yoganup Tramway, 174
London & North Western, 51, 53
Lucy, E.E., 51, 62, 79

Macarthur, 233
McConnell, J.E., 53
"Macgregor", 167
"Major", 203
Manning Wardle, 92, 236
Martin of Gawler, James, 102, 103, 114, 115, 117, 119, 121, 235
Megalong Valley line, 226
"Melbourne", 5
Melbourne–Adelaide Express, 100, 102, 103
Melbourne–Sydney Express, 56
Melbourne and Mount Alexander Railway Co., 15
Melbourne and Hobson's Bay Railway Co., 1
Melbourne and Hobson's Bay United, 15
Melbourne Limited, 68, 80
Melbourne Locomotive and Engineering Works, 235
Mersey tanks, 199, 203–4
Midland Railway Co., 16, 175, 178, 185, 190, 193, 197, 200, 208, 235
Midlander Express, 168
Mikado, 34, 35, 81, 100, 101, 127, 168, 233
Mile End Rail Museum, 105, 108, 110, 114, 115, 116, 120, 122, 124, 128, 206, 208, 214, 215, 223
Minmi ghost railway, 203
Mirls, Solomon, 16
Missouri, Kansas and Texas Railroad, 101
Mogul, 73, 233
Montreal Locomotive Co., 132
Moore, James, 1, 4, 5
Mort & Co., 54, 70, 80
Mount Lyell Mining and Railway Co., 211, 212, 225
Mountain type, 7, 14, 52, 79, 100, 146, 233

249

Munro & Co., David, 43, 235
Museum of Applied Arts & Sciences, Sydney, 60, 69, 96
Museum of Historic Engines, Goulburn, 220–1
museums, 217–26

"Nannies", 62
Nasmyth Wilson & Co., 158, 177, 196, 236
Neilson Reid & Co., 76, 151, 154, 174, 196, 236
Newcastle Flyer, 68
Newport Rail Museum, 221
Newport Workshops, 5, 17, 21, 23, 24, 25, 31, 32, 33, 34, 35, 36, 39, 43, 44, 46, 175, 188, 234
New South Wales Rail Transport Museum, *see* Thirlmere Rail Transport Museum
New South Wales Railways, 49–96, 125–8, 130
New York, New Haven, and Hartford Railroad, 127, 131
New Zealand Railways, 139, 176
Nisbet, W. H., 152
North and Central Australia railways, 97, 127
North Australia Railway, 98, 118, 133
North British Locomotive Co., 27, 35, 76, 113, 126, 177, 178, 179, 180, 186, 210, 211, 234, 236

North-East Dundas Tramway, 138, 148
North Melbourne Carriage & Wagon Shops, 43
Northern Region, 125–136
Nutt, G., 152, 164

"Oberon", 15
Overland, The, 6, 17, 27, 105, 106

Pacific, 7, 27, 64, 67, 68, 69, 100, 101, 106, 108, 141, 142, 154, 161, 163, 175, 176, 177, 178, 179, 180, 232, 233, 209
Parramatta Park Steam Tramway, 94, 95, 96, 217–8
"Pendennis Castle", 200, 201
"Peronne", 214, 215
Perry Engineering Works, 115, 126, 138, 141, 146, 235
Phoenix Foundry, 16, 19, 20, 21, 28, 30, 40, 43, 151, 156, 157, 235
Pichi Richi Railway, 122, 134, 191, 223–4
"Pig", 127
Pinjarra Steam and Hills Railway Preservation Society, 226
Pocono, 233
"Polly", 43
Porter, H.K., 214
Powelltown Tramway, 228
"Pozières," 215
Prairie, 233
private railways, 199–215
Puffing Billy Museum, 208, 212, 215, 222

250

Puffing Billy Preservation Society, 47, 48

Queensland Railways, 127, 150–73, 176, 189, 224, 235

Redbank Museum, 154, 158, 159, 160, 162, 163, 165, 167, 169, 170, 172, 224
Richmond Vale, 199, 203, 204, 205
Roberts, T.S., 121
Robertson and Pemberton, 165
Robertson, Martin and Smith, 1
Robison Bros, 235
Robison Bros, Campbell & Sloss, 235
Robinson, J.G., 204
ROD, 204–5
Rogers Locomotive Works, 237

"Samson", 15
"Sandfly", 132, 133
"Sandridge", 5
Scoular, J., 51
Sharp Stewart, 137, 236
Shay-geared, 228
Shea, F., 100
Shields, F.W., 50
Silverton Tramway, 119, 120, 191, 200, 206, 207, 220, 223
Slaughter, Grunning & Co., 236
Smith, Alfred E., 17, 18, 21, 25
Société Franco-Belge, 121, 122, 170, 236

Société St Leonard, Liège, 236
South Australian Railways, 7, 35, 43, 97, 133, 182, 183, 189, 206, 220, 223, 235
South Maitland Railway Co., 199, 201
Southern Mail, 164
Speight, Richard, 15, 16, 17, 29, 41
"Spirit of Progress", 11, 12, 18, 25, 37
steam tram motor, 95
Stephenson & Co., Robert, 4, 5, 50, 51, 52, 70, 194, 196, 236
Stephenson, George, 49, 50
Stephenson & Hawthorns Ltd, Robert, 143, 176, 193, 234
Sunshine Express, 154
Sydney Express, 19, 25
Sydney Museum of Applied Arts and Sciences, 52
Sydney Railway Company, 50, 53

Tait, Sir Thomas, 17
Tasmanian Government Railways, 7, 97, 122, 137–49, 174, 183, 187, 189, 225
Tasmanian Region, 137–49
Tasmanian Main Line Co., 137
Tasmanian Transport Museum, 144, 212, 225
ten wheeler, 233
Thirlmere Rail Transport Museum, 54, 56, 58, 60,

63, 65, 66, 69, 71, 72, 74, 75, 77, 79, 81, 82, 84, 85, 87, 88, 90, 91, 92, 93, 204, 214, 217
Thompson & Co. (Castlemaine), 21, 135, 235
Thow, W., 51, 59, 66, 76
Timbertown, 226
"Tiny Tim", 154
"Titania", 15
Toowoomba Foundry, 125, 128, 163, 164
tramways, steam, 228
Trans-Australian line, 10, 60, 65, 98, 125, 126, 127, 129, 130
Trans-Australian Express, 97, 132
twelve wheeler, 233

Vale, Henry, 72, 86, 235
Vale & Lacey, 70
Van Diemen Light Railway Society, 143, 225
"Victoria", 5
Victorian Railways, 5, 10, 15–48, 67, 113, 142, 221
Vulcan Foundry, 38, 57, 85, 93, 147, 162, 177, 218, 236, 237

Walkers Ltd, 21, 121, 126, 127, 130, 138, 146, 151, 158, 159, 162, 164, 165, 167, 235
Wallace, James, 50
Webb, W.A., 100, 101, 102, 104, 106, 107, 108, 110
Webster, William, 53
Westcoaster, 210
Western Australian Government Railways, 118, 139, 174–198
Western Australia Transport Museum, *see* Bassendean
wheel classification, 232–3
Whitton, John, 51
Williamstown Rail Museum, 22, 24, 28, 29, 30, 32, 33, 35, 36, 37, 39, 40, 43, 45, 234

"Yarra", 5
Yass Tramway, 91
Yorkshire Engine Co., 158
Young, Harold, 52, 67

Zeehan School of Mines, 210, 212, 225
Zig Zag Railway, 124, 169, 172, 219